Dedications

This book is dedicated to my wife, Jeannie Marie Levinson,
for she knows all the keys to my unconscious mind.

JAY CONRAD LEVINSON

...k is dedicated to my son Kieran – I try to teach him well,
y... ... more every time he speaks. I also dedicate this book to
my littl... ...ter Maria and my parents, Julie and Brian – for anyone
close to me knows that nothing happens in my life without
the support of my family. I wish that Sue, Jim, Margaret and Phyllis
could have read this book.

PAUL HANLEY

About Paul Hanley

Paul Hanley is a true Guerrilla Marketer – ingrained with the principles that have made Guerrilla Marketing acclaimed throughout the world. He is intimately familiar with the secrets, the tactics, the techniques and the history of Guerrilla Marketing.

But perhaps most important, Paul has helped elevate Guerrilla Marketing to a more advanced level. By intertwining marketing and psychology, Paul is at the forefront of still another breakthrough for commerce in the twenty-first century.

His ability to marry the techniques of Neurolinguistic Programming (NLP) to the teachings of Guerrilla Marketing, make him one of the foremost experts on Earth when it comes to advanced marketing techniques and strategies. As a Guerrilla Marketing Master Trainer, Paul has scoured the details of the topic until he not only knows it backwards and forwards, but also is able to train others in the intricacies of advanced Guerrilla Marketing.

JAY LEVINSON

It is truly thrilling to work with Paul Hanley as a professional! Paul brings to the party what's missing most: high-quality standards, critical core values, solid decision-making strategies, and the flexible skill-set to pull it all together successfully.

JOHN LA VALLE,
PRESIDENT OF NLP SOCIETY
CO-AUTHOR OF PERSUASION ENGINEERING

Paul Hanley is without doubt the most amazing marketer that we've ever worked with.

GARY W. BAMFORD
CHIEF EXECUTIVE, BAMFORD GROUP

Paul Hanley's methods are incredible. We have seen a revenue increase on a reduced marketing budget. He is very highly recommended.

TIM GOODACRE
MANAGING DIRECTOR, GOODACRE DESIGN

Paul Hanley is the most advanced marketer and trainer that we've come across. His methods may be considered controversial – but they really do work. We saw an immediate improvement, and plan to continue a programme of ongoing development with him.

JONATHAN BENTLEY
DIRECTOR, IN.HOUSE.MEDIA

Contents

Acknowledgements

Usually, I owe acknowledgements to many people. This time, I owe them to one man – Paul Hanley, who took this book from a bright idea and crafted it into a shining star that will illuminate the path for many businesses. I cannot express how proud and impressed I am with Paul.

JAY CONRAD LEVINSON

I owe a great deal of thanks to very many people. Jay Levinson – for his training, guidance, coaching and generosity ... for without him there is no Guerrilla Marketing. Jeannie Levinson – for the hugs that started this unstoppable force that is the Evolution of Guerrilla Marketing. Mike Burkhardt, Will Reed, Al Lautenslager, Larry Loebig, Amy Levinson and many of the other coaches at the Guerrilla Marketing Association ... the backbone of modern Guerrilla Marketing. Mike Ryan – a client and student, more importantly a long-term friend, and always willing to throw my crap ideas right back at me! Jay Abraham – hugely experienced, hugely successful and hugely generous. The list goes on ... and so will Guerrilla Marketing.

PAUL HANLEY

Foreword

Jay Conrad Levinson has long been the greatest 'no-cost marketing' champion of the small business owner. His past books have all been focused on specific tactical issues – valuable but limiting. This new book does an impressive job of taking one of the most powerful, but complex marketing forces in existence and simplifying, then harnessing it in a highly useable way the small business owner can immediately profit from.

For years I've been a staunch advocate of mastering and understanding how the brain works. With this book, Jay and Paul Hanley have made a great stride to help the ordinary, small business owner use this power in all the marketing, selling and advisory activities they do. Learning the skills presented in this book will automatically multiply the power and success of whatever you do.

JAY ABRAHAM

THE
GUERRILLA
MARKETING
REVOLUTION

Introduction

GUERRILLA MARKETING is the best-selling marketing series in history. Eighteen million copies have been sold in 42 languages, and it has so changed modern commerce that today *Guerrilla Marketing* is required reading on MBA programmes worldwide. Many of the top business schools, universities and colleges have embraced its principles, methods and strategies, agreeing that they demonstrate best practices for modern-day marketing.

Guerrilla Marketing is very different from traditional marketing. In fact there are 20 differences that we speak about in our lectures. We cover these differences throughout the book so for now you only need to understand the largest single difference between them:

Traditional marketing says that you must invest in advertising to ensure marketing success. Guerrilla Marketing says that if you invest time, effort, imagination and some smart psychology-based strategies, you can use the existing 100 Guerrilla Marketing weapons (see page 135) – of which 62 are *free*! (Advertising is only one of the weapons, and it's the most expensive to use, too.) So, despite what traditional marketing organisations will tell you, you *do not* need to have a large marketing budget to compete in your chosen market.

Since its very inception, Guerrilla Marketing has supported the application of psychology to successful marketing. As modern psychology and our understanding of the human brain has advanced, so too has Guerrilla Marketing. The world of commerce is forever changing and marketing must match those changes to keep up, or fall by the wayside. Guerrilla Marketing is constantly identifying new methods, techniques and strategies to lead the way in the twenty-first century. *The Guerrilla Marketing Revolution* details some of the most exciting recent discoveries in Guerrilla Marketing and, most importantly, it introduces new material that will shorten the sales cycle, improve the overall efficiency of your marketing and increase your profits.

We, the authors, have written *The Guerrilla Marketing Revolution* in clear, jargon-free English. It has long been our goal to demystify marketing, whereas traditional marketing organisations would have you believe that it is complex and requires years of experience. We've done all that we can to keep the contents succinct and focused. The language may not be particularly artistic, but profits are more attractive than creative linguistics, and our goal is to help you increase your profits – thus making your balance sheet aesthetically pleasing.

Throughout the book you will notice that the narrative has generally been written in the first person. In some cases this will refer to information offered by Jay Conrad Levinson and in other cases it will refer to materials written by Paul Hanley. To make reading easier, the authors have chosen to simply use the term, 'I'. This is not to hide the identity of the creator, but rather to make the material easier to read, comprehend and apply. Plus, the reality of this book is that both authors have agreed on every word of the content.

One of the key reasons why Guerrilla Marketing has lead the marketing world for so many years is that in traditional marketing opinions, guesswork and 'experience' are the basis upon which marketing campaigns are built. In Guerrilla Marketing the focus is always on the science of psychology and human nature, and this will never change. Guerrilla Marketing will continue to evolve, and we will maintain our resource investment into research of new data provided by the scientific community.

Neurolinguistic Programming (NLP) is finding its way into more lives every day, and Guerrillas are happy to explore any new methods or strategies that increase the marketing arsenal – and NLP does that. NLP is a behavioural model, and set of explicit skills and techniques, founded by Richard Bandler and John Grinder in the early 1970s. Defined as *'the study of the structure of subjective experience'*, NLP studies the patterns or *'programming'* created by the interaction between the brain (*'neuro'*), language (*'linguistic'*) and the body. However, although much of the material in this book has its foundations in NLP, this is not an NLP book. It is true to say that understanding and manipulating behaviour are Guerrilla traits, and NLP offers models to help develop those traits. So, as Dr Richard Bandler, the co-creator of NLP, continues to investigate how far controlling our own minds can go, Guerrillas everywhere will take notice. NLP, and Dr Bandler's most recent creation Neuro-hypnotic Repatterning (NHR), are valuable and powerful weapons in modern marketing, and the more weapons we have in our arsenal, the more flexibility we can apply in our Guerrilla Marketing campaigns.

The Guerrilla Marketing Revolution describes the very latest methods, techniques and strategies that have been developed by Guerrilla Marketing coaches and trainers – the natural evolution of Guerrilla Marketing.

Guerrilla Marketing focuses on providing information in such a way as to affect the decision-making process in prospective purchasers. In short, we seek to influence. To fully understand how we may influence or persuade anyone, we first need to understand how decisions are made. This book describes ways to influence people at the biological level, by physically accessing parts of their brain that they would not usually be aware are part of the decision-making process. You are introduced to techniques and strategies that help people to make decisions more quickly than usual, and more often than not without their awareness of any influence or persuasion.

Some may say that these techniques are 'stealth marketing', or that they have been created to dupe purchasers. This is simply not true. Guerrillas know that such strategies usually result in 'buyer's remorse'. True Guerrillas look to create long-term relationships with their customers and clients, not to just make the sale and move on. If a buyer feels that he has not received great value and exceptional service, a Guerrilla seeks the source of the dissatisfaction and immediately addresses the problem so that it is never repeated. This develops a set of loyal customers. Satisfied customers are easy to find, and loyal customers are rare. The future of profitable marketing is in loyal customers and repeat orders. Guerrillas do not use 'stealth marketing' – they use communication expertise.

The Guerrilla Marketing Revolution presents you with ways of accessing a prospect's mind in order that they can make an informed and honest decision. However, you also learn how to help your audience make decisions without their even being aware that you have done so!

By applying the science of psychology to marketing, Guerrilla Marketing has already shown itself to deliver consistent and eventually predictable results, beyond those usually experienced in traditional marketing. As we rapidly discover more about the human brain and how it works, so we are also learning how decisions are made. The more we understand about the decision-making process at the biological level, the more we can develop methods that appeal to the parts of the brain that make the decisions. As these methods are developed, the systems for influencing the decision-making process become apparent. Sounds easy, doesn't it?

The problem is that the human brain is the most complex formation of mass known to man. Approximately 50 million chemical messages are transmitted every second in the average brain. Huge portions of your brain are not used, and we still don't even understand how some parts work or what they do.

Although progress in this field is rapid, we still have a long way to go. Even if we get to the stage where we can finally say that we fully understand the human brain, we will nonetheless be a long way from completely understanding the decision-making process, because everyone's belief system is unique to them. Effective marketing requires that we influence our audiences as profitably as we can. Effective Guerrilla Marketing requires that we do so using every weapon available to us, including scientific research data.

To market successfully to the unconscious mind requires that you open your own mind. Guerrillas embrace new and unusual techniques and strategies to reach conventional goals. Much of the material in *The Guerrilla Marketing Revolution* will be completely new to you, and your belief system may make you attempt to reject some of it as unimportant, or not applicable to you. Don't let it. It's your brain. Do you want to be a passenger?

Many of the methods discussed will have you question your existing beliefs. This is good – it's called learning. Other methods will excite you, as you identify immediate uses in your own marketing campaigns. Others still will worry you. This may be because they don't seem to be 'quite right', or because they fly in the face of traditional marketing. These are often the methods that actually deliver the most profitable campaigns, as many marketers simply do not have the determination to follow through on the application of non-traditional methods. The motto of the British Special Air Service – 'Who Dares Wins' – perfectly describes the philosophy of Guerrilla Marketing using these methods.

Bear in mind that the techniques and strategies introduced in this book are very powerful, and as such require strong moral ethics in their application. They offer themselves to misuse. I ask that you use them wisely, and with the spirit in which they were created. The power to influence has long been accepted as both a wonderful and a terrible power. Some of the most influential people on Earth have included mass murderers and war criminals. But the individuals who have used their influence for good have all recognised the fact that influence is not about forcing others to do your bidding using slick terms and glib responses, but about better communicating why it would be beneficial for others to comply. Identifying this single trait is fundamental in developing your own power to influence, both in business and in your personal life.

Guerrilla Marketing is, by its very nature, scientific. Science will outdistance guesswork every time. This book is part of the natural evolution in the *Guerrilla Marketing* series. Guerrillas know that the more weapons you have in your arsenal, the more likely it will be that your attacks will possess the flexibility and adaptability required for consistent success. The power to influence the uncon-scious mind is simply the most powerful weapon imaginable, and definitely a weapon worth having in your arsenal. Guerrillas are committed to developing their skills with existing weapons, as well as to identifying new weapons. This book introduces you to a number of new weapons that combine to become the super-weapon that all marketers seek – the power to influence the unconscious mind.

Don't think of a blue elephant. Now, read on.

Why Market to the Unconscious Mind?

I SN'T THAT GREAT? I told you *not* to think of a blue elephant, yet your brain made you do it! It may only have been for a split-second, but your brain created an image of a blue elephant and presented it to you. Now imagine, just imagine; what images could you could place in your clients' minds. With the correct linguistic structure and by applying some simple rules of modern human psychology, the possibilities are limitless.

The conscious and unconscious mind

There are very many books about the structure of the brain. All describe two hemispheres, and a more complex underlying structure of lobes and mapped areas. For the purposes of this book, and indeed for simplicity, we refer to two parts of the brain: the conscious mind and the unconscious mind. The conscious mind has also been referred to as 'the dominant hemisphere', 'vigilant attention' or 'conscious awareness'. At the most basic level, you are using your conscious mind at any time you need to concentrate on something, and you are completely aware of your mental activity.

The unconscious mind is a completely different story. It is what makes you do the things you do – sometimes without even telling you. It processes astonishing amounts of information, and only shares with your conscious mind what it feels is necessary. In fact, it processes so much information that if your conscious mind was exposed to the full load of the decision-making system, it would very likely cause cerebral damage.

The reticular activating system

To prevent this, you have a cluster of brain cells called the reticular activating system (RAS). They act as a fail-safe system, filtering your perceptions. As information is presented to the unconscious mind, the RAS processes the information and decides which information needs to be passed to the conscious mind, based on previous experiences and the established belief system.

Information that the RAS considers to be of high importance is transferred rapidly. For example, when you put your hand on a hot object you are made consciously aware of pain. This is the unconscious mind's way of telling you to stop it. You pull your hand away without conscious effort – that is the unconscious protecting you from physical harm. It is only after you are removed from physical harm that you feel the pain message. However, information that the RAS considers to be of low importance is passed to your conscious awareness much more slowly, if at all. This explains why learning to play golf, tightrope walking and long division are so difficult for many people. The RAS does not recognise these things as important for most of us.

As we learn to do difficult things, they become easier to do. This is because the RAS recognises that any repeated activity must have an increased level of significance, or we wouldn't do it. The result is that it permits additional resource to the learning process.

The great news for Guerrillas is that the RAS can be reprogrammed, and marketing to the unconscious mind does that.

Marketing to the unconscious mind

There are five essential reasons why Guerrillas should market to the unconscious mind and the brief demonstration with the blue elephant (see page 6) clearly displays the first.

1. The brain uses images to help the conscious mind understand

Every word in your natural language is represented in your mind by an image. Every sound you ever hear is associated with an image in your mind. Every feeling you have ever experienced, or can imagine experiencing, is also represented by an image, or images, in your mind.

The way in which you experience the image, and indeed the absolute contents of the image, are what make it personal to you. For example, when your brain created the image of the blue elephant, it may have been a still image, or it may have been a moving image. You may have seen a blue elephant in a jungle, or a zoo, or some other place. It may have been dark blue or light blue. Your blue elephant is exactly that – *your* blue elephant.

Traditional marketing acknowledges that people create images in their minds, but doesn't truly understand how or why, or indeed how to use that critical information. There have been marketing campaigns designed to create wonderful visualisations in people's minds. Many advertisements actually ask that you 'imagine' something. The only way to imagine anything is to create an image in your mind. So in fact traditional marketing is part of the way there. However, what traditional marketing has failed to understand is that no one will have the same visualisation that the advertisement designer experienced. His or her blue elephant is not the same as yours. It may be slightly different, or hugely different, but it will be different.

The human brain may be considered a very complex computer. As you absorb information throughout your life, it processes, prioritises and stores everything ready for future access. We now know that the majority of the filing processes are conducted during our sleep, specifically during periods of sleep known as Rapid Eye Movement (REM). These periods occur approximately every 90 minutes, for between 15 and 30 minutes. This is the time when you dream. Your dreams are a visualisation of information that your body has absorbed throughout the day, and information that your mind has been processing, often trying to associate meaning to sights, sounds and feelings that have been experienced but not fully understood. When you experience a dream, you are witnessing your brain's filing processes.

It follows that, as is the case with any computer, you cannot be running the programme and editing it at the same time. This is the reason why we need sleep. The brain gets to a point where it realises it has collected huge amounts of data and needs to begin the filing process, so you become tired. The computer is essentially preparing for back-up. In the human life cycle, babies soak up more information than any other age group. The result is that they require more sleep. The more information they take in, the more sleep they need. This is true of adults, too. If you spend a large amount of concentration on learning something new, you become tired more quickly than you would usually expect.

Although the brain is like a computer, it is not like your PC or Mac. These types of computer store an image file in a single place. Your brain, on the other hand, stores image data in many places. For example, when you read or hear the word 'elephant' the brain immediately creates an image of an elephant. So where does the brain get the information to create the image? Well, the fact that an elephant is grey is stored in one place. The fact that it is big is stored somewhere else. The fact that it moves slowly is stored somewhere else again. The fact that it has a trunk is stored somewhere else too. There are hundreds of features that enable you to identify an elephant, and each is stored in a different part of your brain. The quickest and easiest way for your brain to help you understand what 'elephant' means is to create an image for you.

Guerrillas know that to market to the unconscious mind you must always bear in mind that no two people will have exactly the same images, regardless of how specific your creation of the visualisation may be. Therefore intentionally implanting images in your prospects' minds should be a component part of the message, but not the message.

2. The unconscious mind is much smarter than the conscious mind

This next essential reason why Guerrillas should market to the unconscious mind may hurt your feelings a little, until you've read the explanation.

As you are reading this book your unconscious mind is looking after you. Right now your unconscious mind is monitoring and controlling your body temperature, your immune system, your balance, your spatial awareness, your breathing, your heart beat, your circulation, your bodily fluids and your five senses. Most importantly, it does all this without bothering your conscious awareness. It tells you when to blink, and when your body needs more oxygen, or water or carbohydrates. How often are you aware of these messages? Not very often. Anything that you have ever considered to be instinct or a reflex action is actually unconscious system management.

The unconscious mind recognises its superior performance over the conscious mind and as a result tends to protect it by only providing information that the conscious mind demands, or requires for comprehension. Even then, the unconscious mind is often selective in the data transfer, regularly choosing to 'drip feed' the information to prevent overload. This may be because the information challenges existing beliefs, or simply because the nature of the data is complex.

The unconscious mind rarely overrides decisions made by your conscious mind, even though it is more intelligent. For example, when a smoker picks up a cigarette the unconscious mind says, 'Cigarettes are not good for your health. They're going to kill you.' Then the conscious mind argues, 'But I like them.' There are thousands of people who regularly use their credit cards for purchases that they don't need, and probably can't really afford. Their unconscious might say, 'You can't afford it. Your credit card bill will cripple you financially at the end of the month, and you're paying high interest rates.' Then the conscious mind pipes up, 'But I want it.'

This type of interaction between the conscious and unconscious is called internal dialogue. It is when you actually hear voices in your head – which brings us to point three.

3. The unconscious mind controls your internal dialogue

Let's clarify something right now; everyone hears voices in their head. This isn't due to schizophrenia or any other psychological problem. It's because of how your brain manages thinking. We call it internal dialogue. Even now as you read this page, you can hear yourself reading it. Your brain is making you sound out each sentence, because the majority of the language that you use is verbal, and writing is only a graphical representation of a word.

Consider this: if you went to see a psychiatrist in the 1960s and told them that you could hear voices in your head, they would have heard a voice in their own head saying, 'This person has psychological problems,' and you would probably have been treated with drugs!

Now, however, we know that internal dialogue is perfectly natural, and recognising its influence on the decision-making process is an excellent marketing weapon. Guerrillas seek to utilise every advantage offered, and the opportunity offered by utilising language to stimulate positive internal dialogue is a very powerful weapon.

Your prospects will experience internal dialogue, whether it is driven by you or not. Your goal as a Guerrilla should be to bring about positive states in your prospects, because people in poor or negative states make bad decisions. How many people do you know who have finished one relationship, been miserable, and then gone straight into another bad relationship? We read every day about people who have had financial problems that have spiralled out of control. These people are in negative states, due to the stress and worry of debt. Then they make financial decisions while in these states, and wonder why there is no improvement.

If a prospect is in a positive state when they are making a purchasing decision, they are much less likely to experience buyer's remorse. A client who is happy with their purchase is also more likely to purchase from you again than one who isn't, and Guerrillas always seek repeat business and referrals. Many studies have been conducted to identify how many customers would buy from you again, if you offered a similar or related product at a similar price. The answer found by all was about 34 per cent. Have you any idea of the expense in marketing to an audience one-third the size of your existing client base? It's substantial, when you recognise that you can market to your existing clients for free, and 34 per cent are likely to purchase from you.

For many years, some trainers have suggested that one of the strongest motivators to purchase is highlighting 'pain', and building a marketing strategy upon the prospect's wish to avoid that 'pain'. We now know that there are better ways to motivate the purchasing decision, and the majority of these methods require that the prospect is in a positive state, rather than buying to avoid discomfort. Indeed, the question should be whether a person avoiding a consequence is being motivated to purchase, or being forced to do so. It's a thin line.

Guerrillas focus not only on satisfying customers, but also on retaining them. Customers who feel that they have been backed into a corner to make a purchasing decision are less likely to buy from you again, when compared to customers who are given many options and freedom of choice. Guerrillas aim to present options, and to respect customers in their ability to make intelligent and informed decisions.

To move prospects to positive states and keep them there, Guerrillas use language, imagery and the Guerrilla Marketing weapons that produce constructive messages, which in turn bring about positive internal dialogue. Propulsion is a more powerful marketing weapon than aversion. For example, traditional marketing might offer the very negative, 'Without a security alarm, your home and family are at risk.' Guerrilla Marketing prefers the more positively motivating, 'Sleep soundly in the safe knowledge that you have protected your home and family.'

Some marketers simply fail to consider internal dialogue. Rhetorical questions often bring about negative internal dialogue. Everyone has seen poorly constructed advertisement headlines along the lines of, 'Would you like to earn more?' When we read these headlines, our unconscious takes over and we hear our own voice in our head saying things like:

'Of course I would, idiot.'

'Don't insult my intelligence.'

'No. I want to work longer hours for less money!'

Guerrillas hear themselves say, 'Who writes this stuff? I need to get an appointment with their boss. They should be a client!'

What were you saying to yourself after you last made a purchase of substantial value? If you were still questioning whether you should have made the purchase or not, then the marketing process was not complete, and your internal dialogue had not been considered. If, on the other hand, you were happy and excited about the purchase, then your internal dialogue would have sounded different. When we suffer buyer's remorse, the tonality of our internal dialogue is very different from when we are in a positive state.

You may have told your friends and family about a purchase you are about to make and they have tried to discourage you. Did their voice tonality sound particularly enthusiastic? Was there a supportive tone to their, 'That is such a terrible waste of money. Are you on drugs?' Did you feel the heady grip of eagerness to get to the store? Of course not. The same is true of internal dialogue. If the dialogue is not positive and fails to build excitement, then the purchasing decision is not ready to be made.

4. The unconscious mind can understand and link multiple messages

Over the past 30 or 40 years, many scientific research papers have been published on the abilities of conscious awareness. Although various opinions have been offered, they generally all agree that the conscious mind struggles with more than three or four issues at any given time. This is easily demonstrated. If you have two people talking to you at the same time, you may just be able to comprehend what both people are saying. If a third person is added, it becomes increasingly difficult, and your unconscious mind steps in to help you start recognising linguistic patterns – so you don't need to hear every word spoken by all three speakers to make sense of the conversation. If a fourth speaker is thrown in, it is very unlikely that you will make any sense of the four conversations.

Your unconscious mind can manage millions of functions, and in this respect is very much like a super-computer. There is a huge difference, however, between the human brain and any computer on Earth. The brain can associate data streams based on relevance, disregarding unimportant information, and make a decision based on historical data, possible future outcomes and experience. A computer can only make decisions by evaluating all available information, as it can't decide what is relevant and what is not. Guerrillas choose to market to the unconscious mind because they can simultaneously appeal to several parts of the mind, with multiple messages. This in turn helps to speed the decision-making process.

Guerrillas also know that the unconscious mind can construct even the most tenuous of links, associating information sets to build a more detailed understanding for the conscious mind. As a rule of thumb, allowing the unconscious to create links for itself is more productive than giving direct instructions. In order to accept direct instructions, the brain requires trust in the sender of the message, which is called 'rapport'. Creating rapport can take days, weeks or even months. It also requires a very specific set of communication tools (see page 46).

Giving the unconscious a set of marketing messages that it can then assemble to produce a single, coherent marketing overview usually results in a more rapidly devised and committed decision. After all, the unconscious trusts its own judgement better than any direct instruction from someone else. Typically, when marketers present marketing messages as direct instructions, the conscious mind will second guess the decision – and remember, the conscious isn't that smart!

5. The unconscious mind makes decisions before consulting the conscious

Guerrillas know that it is possible to enable a prospect to make a decision, before they are consciously aware that a decision has been made. This is done by marketing to the unconscious mind.

Here is one of the most important lessons you will ever learn about the human brain: the unconscious mind cannot work slowly – it can only work at high speed. Your brain is a huge network, packed full of electrical impulses and chemical messages, all of which move very quickly indeed. Have you ever tried to slow down electricity? The signals are transmitted around your brain at very high speeds because of the huge number of neural pathways available to manage the signals. In Guerrilla Marketing the aim is to build neural pathways that permit easy repeat access. I present details on how to do this later (see page 67).

The unconscious mind is most comfortable, and indeed efficient, when working at high capacity. Furthermore, it actually tries to find short cuts when processing, so that it can speed up its data management and decision strategies. When seeking short cuts, the unconscious mind makes multiple attempts to identify relevant associations in any, or all, of the data sets. Why is this important to Guerrillas? Well, we know that when marketing to the unconscious mind, we can be more subtle than we would be if we were using traditional marketing methods. We can make use of language patterns including presupposition, generalisation, ambiguity and deletion (see pages 37–45 for detailed discussion on each of these tools).

Since the unconscious mind works at such high speed, and is so much more sensitive to subtlety than the conscious mind, it always recognises models, associations and patterns ahead of the conscious. This is an excellent weapon that very few marketers seem to understand, and Guerrillas deliberately utilise.

It is now accepted that mental processes are essentially unconscious, and the conscious mind responds to these processes. Knowing this, why would we want to target the conscious mind for marketing purposes? Traditional marketing has thus far failed to identify that all decisions are first made by the unconscious, and instead chooses to throw large budgets at campaigns based on repetitive messaging. This is an expensive and inefficient means of marketing.

For example, a traditional marketing campaign trying to sell training courses to sales managers might read 'Do you have problems closing new business?' If the prospective client reads this and thinks 'No' then the conversation is over, and the remainder of the copy is unlikely to be read.

For Guerrilla Marketing in the same scenario, the copy might read 'When do you have problems closing new business?' This requires the prospective client's unconscious mind to go through a personal derivation to recall a time when he did have a problem closing new business, because until he does he cannot fully understand the question. This derivation builds rapport, because as the image of the problem is created, the conscious awareness thinks, 'Wow! This company really understands me.'

Have you ever made a decision that proved to be incorrect, and suffered 'I knew it' remorse? If you knew it, why did you make the decision you made? In the most basic terms, your conscious mind decided to override the decision made by the unconscious. Frankly, considering the greater resources available to the unconscious mind and its processing abilities, it's incredible that we ever allow our conscious mind to make a decision at all. Just stop and think for a moment. When you suffered 'I knew it' remorse, that meant that you were arguing with yourself, in your mind. Makes you think, doesn't it?

A recent documented case on UK television described how the unconscious mind of a fire brigade officer saved the lives of six of his colleagues. The fire crew in question were called to a large warehouse fire in Nottingham. Upon arrival, the crew surveyed the warehouse and the order was given to enter the premises to fight the fire. After two or three minutes, the officer had an uneasy sensation about the whole event and ordered his team out of the premises. They argued that everything was OK, but he insisted that they vacate the building immediately.

Within 30 seconds of clearing the warehouse there was an enormous explosion, and the area where the firemen had been working became a ferocious inferno. The team would undoubtedly have been killed if they had remained in the building – and they owe their lives to the unconscious mind of their officer.

When the officer was interviewed an hour after the event, he still could not explain why he had made the decision that he did. However, the next day he was able to detail exactly why he had instructed his team to vacate the premises. Without being consciously aware, his unconscious had noticed that the smoke coming from the fire was orange, not black, and he could see air being sucked back into the fire. When his unconscious also noticed that the fire was very quiet, and there were few of the familiar crackling noises associated with regular burning, it began an important comparison process. It considered the hundreds of fires that the officer had previously experienced, added the material collated in training and compared all this data with the situation it faced. The result was that it identified a backdraft – one of the most dangerous types of fire, known for violent explosions.

Due to the urgency of the situation, the unconscious did not give the conscious mind all the details, or the chance to argue. Instead, the conscious was simply told, 'There is danger. You must remove your men.' The officer was not aware why, but due to the intensity of the message, the conscious complied without question. Only after the event did the unconscious mind decide to share its reasoning with the conscious awareness of the officer.

As Guerrillas, we know that we must market to the unconscious mind. However, we also need to keep the conscious mind actively involved. It is rare for the conscious mind to be happy to be a passenger. This is due to ego. Guerrillas know that marketing always needs to be mindful of ego, and occasionally needs to nurse an ego, too. The unconscious regularly battles with the ego, so ideally Guerrillas seek the understanding and compliance of both unconscious and conscious minds.

Traditional marketing has targeted the conscious minds of prospects, choosing to ignore the thousands of scientific papers and research studies, which clearly show that the unconscious mind makes decisions both before, and also more quickly than the conscious mind.

Guerrilla Marketing has produced the ongoing success that it has because Guerrillas know that marketing to the unconscious mind is the route to rapid, yet stable purchasing decisions. Ordinary marketers don't know this – which is why they are ordinary.

CHAPTER 2

Appeal to Your Prospects' Unconscious

B EFORE WE EVEN get started on the new methods and strategies we've developed in Guerrilla Marketing, you need to be very clear on how the brain works – specifically, how it manages images and messages presented through marketing. There are many myths about this very subject, so this chapter clarifies the facts, and shows you how to best use them to your advantage.

Words as a marketing tool

I'm sure you've seen the many books, ebooks and papers that claim to contain 'words that sell' or 'phrases guaranteed to sell'. Be very clear on this – words are just words. Nothing else. They have no hidden powers. Words are just a cluster of scribbles and sounds that we use to demonstrate what we mean. Words do not sell. However, the way in which we use words can make a huge difference to any marketing message or campaign.

What you will learn in this chapter is that words are a catalyst. Words are tools that we use to access or create associations. The associations are usually already in place in the minds of your prospects, and the skilful use of words can activate the association – thus enabling the purchasing decision.

Stop and think about it. Take the example of the word 'chair'. This is a word that we associate with a four-legged object, designed for sitting upon. As you just read the word 'chair', your brain created an image of a chair for you, didn't it? OK, so that's your chair. Remember the blue elephant (see page 6)? Well it works the same way with every word in your vocabulary. You have your own associations and images for each and every word.

Try this. Think of a chair. You now have an image of a chair in your mind – your chair. Now, think of a chair with blue stripes on it. You will notice two things – firstly, it's more difficult to visualise it, isn't it? When I gave you the freedom to create the chair of your choice, your brain did it in the tiniest fraction of a second. However, when I violated your chair by insisting that it was a certain colour, your brain took longer to create that image. Suddenly, your chair wasn't your chair any more. It was a chair with blue stripes.

Secondly, it feels different when you create the chair with blue stripes. Some people add the blue stripes to their own chair, while others create a totally different chair. Which did you do? It's not important, but it is worth noticing. What is important is that you are aware that when your images are violated or restricted, you feel physically different. The word 'chair' suddenly feels different.

Effective marketing takes into account that people can be made to feel differently through the use, or misuse, of language. In Guerrilla Marketing we are very particular about the language we use, because we know that it is not the words but the associations that control the success of a marketing message, so every word is intentional.

Surface and deep structures

When considering language, there are two parts of the equation that we take into account:

1. Surface structure

2. Deep structure

The surface structure, at the most basic level, is the words. The physical markings that we read represent the surface structure of a sentence. The deep structure, on the other hand, is the meaning that we draw from the surface structure, based on our background and experiences.

As an example, 'John is running' represents the surface structure of a sentence. To determine the deep structure requires a derivation, using personal experiences. Using the example above, a typical deep structure might be that a noun called 'John' is presently conducting a verb action called 'running'. It is also fair, and probable, to assume that John is male, alive and capable of conducting the 'running'. This is not necessarily true, as John could be female, but based on a personal derivation, very few people would expect John to be female.

It is also very likely that the derivation will continue to attempt to answer the questions such as 'Why is John running, and from whom?' and 'Where is John running to and from?' Who would have believed that three little words could create so many questions?

The visual, auditory and kinesthetic systems

To help us maximise our persuasive abilities in Guerrilla Marketing, we have adopted some of Dr Bandler's NLP model (see page 36) and focused on the three main representational systems – visual, auditory and kinesthetic.

NLP has been around for 30 years and is essentially a way of describing what happens in people's minds. It is a complex science built around simple observations, and this is not the place to detail how and why NLP will help you. Dr Bandler and his colleagues have spent many years perfecting the models and systems that he identified. Please read as many of his books as you can (see Resources, page 170), as this will add a huge number of weapons to your existing arsenal, and he can explain his models much better than I can.

The three main representational systems are demonstrated verbally and non-verbally, depending on a person's state.

Visual states

A person who is visually dominant or in a visual state will tend to use visual phrases:

- 'I see what you mean.'

- 'I can't picture that.'

- 'Can you show me the way?'

- 'That appears to be right.'

A visual person will also tend to speak quickly, in short bursts. Very typically they will breathe very high in their chest, and regularly look upwards to access images in their mind.

Here's an example – take a moment and consider this question: 'What colour is your front door?' You just looked up and created an image of your front door. It may have been only for a fraction of a second, but your eyes looked upwards to enable you to access an image from your mind. If you didn't, and some people don't, then you probably stared straight ahead and defocused your eyes to create the image in your mind. Either way, you had the image of your front door in your mind, and for a brief moment you were in a visual state.

Auditory states

Auditory dominant people, and people in auditory states, tend to use words and phrases that demonstrate a preference for sound-based presentation:

- 'I hear you loud and clear.'

- 'The name rings a bell.'

- 'To tell the truth, I'm not sure.'

- 'Listen up!'

Auditory people tend to speak slower than visual people, and breathe from the centre of the chest. Auditory people are often articulate – almost bathing you in the words they choose to use. It is a common misconception in body language that folded arms are a barrier; in reality this body posture is often that of an auditory person giving you their full attention. People in an auditory state also tend to look from side to side. This is how they access sounds they have heard before, or are trying to create in their mind.

For example, take your time now and try this: remember your favourite song or tune. Notice where your eyes go. Don't manufacture a movement – just go back to a time when you remember hearing the song or tune. You will notice that you can hear the sounds in your head. You've just been in an auditory state.

Kinesthetic states

A person who is kinesthetically dominant or in a kinesthetic state will generally use words and phrases that describe feelings, emotions and actions:

- 'I'll lay my cards on the table.'

- 'I'll get in touch with them.'

- 'It doesn't feel right.'

- 'I don't follow you.'

The speaking pace of a person in a kinesthetic state is typically slower than that of someone in a visual or auditory state, and they will also tend to breathe deeply from the diaphragm. In a manner that is frustrating for visual and auditory dominant people, kinesthetically dominant people often insert long pauses into their speech – almost considering what they are saying as they say it.

Do you remember the last time you were really cold? Do you remember now where you first felt the cold, and how it moved through your body? You have just been in a kinesthetic state.

Now you are equipped with a small set of tools that can help you identify the preferred representational system of a prospect, and you have personally been moved from one representational system to another. (You've seen your front door, you've heard your favourite song and you've remembered feeling cold.) Reading this chapter has enabled you to see how easy it is to move someone from their dominant state to a more desirable state. Manipulation? You bet. In the *Concise Oxford English Dictionary* the definition of 'manipulation' is described as the ability to 'handle masterfully'. Can you think of any better way to handle your prospects? Guerrillas always handle their prospects and clients masterfully.

Marketing's most powerful and best-kept secret?

Now you are going to be introduced to one of the most important discoveries in sales and marketing psychology to date. This discovery is incredibly important, and yet has been hardly publicised – with good reason. If everyone knew this one fact then all sales and marketing campaigns would be more efficient. There are a small number of sales and marketing professionals who know this, and are already using it to its maximum potential. More importantly, you can read this now and then apply it immediately. Sit back and learn one of the most profitable strategies in this book:

> **A prospect cannot make a purchasing decision until they have experienced a kinesthetic sensation regarding the time after the purchase.**

This has huge implications on everything you are doing now. Until your prospects have imagined how it will feel to own your product, or use your service, they won't buy. Check your sales copy and marketing collateral. Is it primarily visual? Do you use auditory terms throughout? Do you close your copy with a call to action, using kinesthetic terms?

A large semiconductor company in the UK had a brilliant sales manager. His team were by far the most productive in the market, even though the market was supposed to be in depression. Every month the salesmen each exceeded personal and team targets, and all made great commissions. The sales manager regularly held sales meetings with his team to discuss common objectives, and ways in which they could improve performance.

I was given the opportunity to study the sales manager's training material and scripts. Very quickly I realised that he clearly understood that a prospect cannot make a purchasing decision until they have experienced a kinesthetic sensation regarding the post-purchase period. Many sales and marketing managers have developed a 30-second script introducing the company and its main unique selling proposition (USP). This is often called an 'elevator script'. However, this particular manager had taken the brief script idea one step further. He had created a set of scripts for his team. One script was for moving a visually dominant person to a kinesthetic state. Another script was for moving an auditory person to a kinesthetic state. His team were given the scripts, and required to learn them.

The scripts were brilliant. Each introduced the idea: 'Imagine ahead twelve months from now'. Immediately, the prospects would be creating images of the future in their minds. Then, using the present tense, the script continued: 'Your production is up, and your waste is at an all-time low. You feel like your job is less manic and you can go about your professional duties, safe in the knowledge that your department's performance is at an all-time high. Now that's an easy decision to make, wasn't it?' Did you notice the change of tense at the end? By changing the tense and completing the sentence in the past tense, you construct a presupposition that the decision has already been made, and usually the listener will accept this as true, without question. The listener will also move into the future in their mind, so he or she can look back at the decision. Use this technique sparingly, as sticklers for grammar may notice unless it is delivered in an expert manner. The fact is that the rules of English grammar and the rules of Guerrilla Marketing language patterns are not always the same.

Make buyers feel better

In every piece of marketing material where you seek to gain a purchasing decision, and in every piece of sales collateral, you should be building images and describing how the purchaser's life will *feel* better after the purchase. This has two benefits:

1. **It reduces buyer's remorse** If a prospect goes into their mind, imagines how life will be after the purchase and still goes ahead with the purchase, then it is very unlikely that they will later regret the purchase. On the other hand, if the buyer has never imagined their future after the purchase, and makes the purchase, then there is a realistic possibility of buyer's remorse (see also page 55).

2. **It can inoculate against objections** It is a fact that throughout your life your body will be attacked by diseases and viruses. To combat this, as a child (and indeed as an adult, if travelling abroad) you are given injections to aid your immune system. These injections are called inoculations. It is also a fact that throughout your sales and marketing career you will be bombarded by objections. So why not inoculate against these too? You know that you will get objections thrown at you, so why not prepare in advance? Inoculations are not glib, rehearsed responses – as presented in many sales and marketing books. Guerrillas use communications expertise, not rehearsed responses. Read about inoculations in Chapter 4 (see page 63).

Do you *really* understand what you are marketing?

So you now know how to identify which of the three major representational systems your prospect prefers, and you know that you need to move your prospect to a kinesthetic state. Now the important question is whether you really understand what you are marketing.

You are not marketing products.
You are not marketing services.
You are not marketing your organisation.
You are selling feelings.

I can already hear the purists saying, 'Marketing and sales are not the same.' Well, the truth is that marketing is about creating profit, and the only true means of measuring marketing success is profit. So how is that different from sales? Do you measure sales success according to the number of visits you make in a week, how many outbound sales calls are made in a day or how many enquiries you get on the website? You might, but you shouldn't. There are companies that do, and they're not as profitable as they should be. The only function of a sales department is to create profit. We need to be very clear on this; sales is a component part of the marketing process. Marketing is not an event – it is a cycle.

OK, so now we're selling feelings, using the preferred representational system of our prospect. We know that we need to move them to a kinesthetic state so that they can make the purchasing decision. How do we move a prospect from one state to another? There are a large number of methods, and Guerrillas use whatever weapons they have to hand. In this book you are introduced to the simplest method, since simple weapons are the easiest to master.

Expanding a business

I once had a client who sold audio equipment to DJs and nightclubs. His showroom looked amazing and he had sent his sales staff on a three-day training course – although not mine. His problem was simple; he wasn't selling enough equipment to remain profitable. (Amazing showrooms can cost amazing amounts of money to build and maintain.) He asked me to study his salesmen, review his marketing collateral and provide consultancy on expanding his business.

The first observation I made was that his showroom *looked* terrific, so that would appeal to the visually dominant visitors. Conversely, he only had a small area available to listen to the performance of the equipment, and it was not signposted – visitors had to ask where it was. This alienated visitors who were in an auditory dominant state. Astonishingly, there was no area set aside for visitors to physically handle the equipment. Now, DJs are typically very tactile and are more sensitive to mechanical movement than most people. For most of their working lives they are in the dark, thus limiting their visual dominance, and they need to have very strong auditory skills, but almost every DJ that I've worked with has had very developed kinesthetic skills. Many can tell from touch whether a record deck is flat or not, even where the discrepancy is only a millimetre or two. We decided to employ a three-step process.

Step 1

Step 1 involved putting up large signs offering everyone the opportunity to listen to any piece of equipment in use, with directions to the allotted area. The area set aside for listening to the equipment was filled with the best-quality speakers, leads and amplifiers, utilising the latest technologies. No expense was spared to ensure crystal-clear sound, with crisp treble and a deep bass. At all times, even when no visitors were in the area, a specially selected set of music tracks was playing. The tracks had been selected to show the systems' excellence in handling all music types, from 160 beats per minute dance music to orchestral classical.

Step 2

In Step 2, the same area was equipped with equipment that visitors could handle. Top of the range systems were installed, with as many knobs and lights, in as many different styles as could be managed. Suddenly, this area appealed to kinesthetic, auditory and visually dominant visitors.

DJs could get a *feel* for the record decks, and could even *see* the lights that showed them what their music *sounded* like. (Have you ever considered that? A graphic equaliser is a piece of audio equipment designed to show you what your music sounds like. That is visual dominance in the extreme.) The whole showroom was a grotto of sensory overload, and I was excited every time I visited it.

Step 3

Step 3 involved some simple sales training for the staff – all the staff. We began with the basics. Each member of staff was shown how to identify visitors' preferred representational systems. Then we developed three sets of scripts, which were dependent on the preferred system. Each script utilised a minimum of three statements confirming the preferred state to build rapport, then a statement or two to move the visitor to a kinesthetic state. For example:

1. **Visitor:** 'Hi. Can I have a *look* at that amplifier, please?'

2. **Staff:** 'Sure. Let me *show* you it. There, doesn't it *look* great?'

3. **Visitor:** 'Yes, it *looks* amazing.'

4. **Staff:** 'Where do you *see* it best fitting in your system?'

5. **Visitor:** 'It would be our primary amplifier.'

6. **Staff:** 'It's going to be your primary amplifier? Now I *follow* you. You'll *feel* great working with this. It'll *fit* right in with your system. It's so easy to *use*, you're going to *get to grips* with this in no time. You want me to *go ahead* and pack it for you?'

7. **Visitor:** 'Yes, OK. *Go ahead.*'

Although this may seem obvious when the representational systems are marked, this script gave the sales staff the ability to move a visually dominant visitor to a kinesthetic state, where they could become a customer. Let's go through exactly how the script works:

- **Line 1** This is obviously a visually dominant opening. Why would a visitor want to see an amplifier? It doesn't move when it's working, and will usually sit in a cupboard where nobody can see it.

- **Line 2** The staff member matches the visitor's representational system and offers two visual responses, instantly beginning the rapport-building process. Within two sentences the visitor feels that the staff member understands them.

- **Line 3** The visitor confirms that they are still in a visually dominant state.

- **Line 4** The staff member offers another visual statement to further build rapport, assuring the visitor of understanding. This also forces the visitor to create an image of a future where they own the amplifier, and it is installed in the system.

- **Line 5** The visitor offers information in the future tense.

- **Line 6** The staff member repeats the visitor's information, but subtly makes it a confirmation statement – changing 'it would be' to a much more definite 'it's going to be'. Also, by using the correct intonation and analogue marking (both covered in following chapters, see page 37) the staff member adds the word 'Now' from the subsequent sentence. This makes the message to the unconscious, 'It's going to be your primary amplifier now.' The staff member continues with five further kinesthetic references to maintain an unconscious inclination for comfort in a kinesthetic state.

- **Line 7** Unconsciously, the visitor has been paced and then led to a kinesthetic state, and is ready to buy. They indicate this by making a kinesthetic statement.

Similar scripts were developed for auditory-dominant visitors and kinesthetic, too – they also need rapport building, even though they're in a kinesthetic state. Due to the combination of the demonstration area, improved signage, better-trained staff and a well-balanced set of Guerrilla Marketing weapons, in one month profits exceeded the total of the previous 12 months. Why? Were the staff members misusing their skills? Far from it. In fact, they each became better communicators simply by noticing the preferred representational system of visitors. The result was that they were better able to display understanding to visitors, family and friends – and better able to get across their own message, too.

In summary, you can now sell feelings, using the preferred representational system of your prospect, moving them to a kinesthetic state and helping them to become a customer.

Smart, low-cost marketing – building a brand

I want to tell you about another DJ called Harry who is not only a good friend, but also created a marketing model that displays excellence in Guerrilla Marketing. More importantly for you, it shows how a small investment can build a profitable brand, and can link representational systems.

Typically, DJs at the top dance clubs are young and trendy, and aware that their shelf life is not expected to be very long. Harry, however, is the exception to almost every rule surrounding DJs. Harry is in his late forties. He's short and of a 'portly' build. He would never claim to be trendy – but he is a great businessman and an excellent marketer. Recognising the huge number of young DJs just waiting to take his job, Harry decided to do things that were smarter than anything anyone else would devise. He did two things that guaranteed his success:

1. He invested in technology. Harry was one of the first DJs to use a laptop computer to store, mix and play music. When he first started to use a laptop, DJs everywhere laughed at him, accusing him of using technology to support his lack of mixing talent. (Harry could always mix, but he simply felt that computers could do it better.) Today, the majority of DJs are moving to this technology, but they will always be catching up – as Harry continues to invest, to protect his advantage.

2. He invested in lollipops. Whenever clubbers requested that Harry play a particular tune, he would oblige and offer a lol-

lipop. Soon word spread and Harry was giving out 300 lollipops a night. Stop and think about this. Harry would buy lollipops in bulk, so each lollipop would cost approximately one penny. Thus for an investment of only three or four pounds per night, Harry was building a strong product-supported brand. This brand has got stronger and stronger. Harry is now so well known for his lollipops that on the evenings he isn't working, the replacement DJs receive hundreds of requests for lollipops.

Harry is one of the most successful DJs in the town. He's definitely been around the longest, and he plays three of four nights every week in the town's largest club. Against all the odds, and with tens of young, potential replacements snapping at his heals, he has continued to strengthen his position, and frankly shows no sign of slowing down. His success is due to smart marketing. Harry recognises that investing in his position will protect it, and in true Guerrilla style he has made a small investment in lollipops work to his advantage.

Marketing to the Masses

So far the techniques and strategies you've been introduced to, have been focused on individuals or small groups, but what about larger scale marketing?' Marketing to the masses is, in fact, *not* good Guerrilla Marketing ... unless you recognise that marketing to the masses is actually marketing to lots of individuals.

In the first instance, all marketing should be personal. Letters that are addressed to 'The Sales Director' are very rarely read. Let's face it, if you can't be bothered to find out the name of the person you are targeting, are you really likely to provide an attentive service?

For this reason, you should instead focus on personalised interaction, driven by the language skills that we present to you in later chapters. The skills presented in these chapters work very well with individuals, small companies and large organisations, but only when you target groups as a collection of individuals.

Remembering clients' representational systems

Guerrillas know that information about existing clients and prospects is worth millions of pounds, euros and dollars. Add a field in your client database for information regarding the preferred representational system of each and every contact you have, at every organisation. Next time you call a contact, consult your database first to remind yourself of the contact's preferred system. If the client is visually dominant, you could open with, 'Hi, Michael. I *saw* an article in the *Financial Times* and thought you might be interested.' If the client is auditory dominant, you could start with, 'Hi, Michael. I *heard* about an article in the *Financial Times* and thought you might be interested.' If the client is kinesthetic dominant, 'Hi, Michael. I *felt* you might be interested in this story from the *Financial Times*' would probably work best.

As Guerrilla Marketing has evolved, Guerrillas have begun to understand that although words are only the catalyst, the conscious and unconscious associations triggered by words are powerful weapons. Guerrillas embrace powerful weapons, but a weapon is only as powerful as its user's knowledge allows. A magnificent weapon can be hugely inefficient if the user doesn't understand the market, the message or the thrust of the campaign.

An understanding of how to create a fulfilling sensory experience for a prospect is a wonderful skill. This chapter has introduced a set of tools that will help you perfect this skill. To further enhance your persuasive abilities, you need to learn how to use language to your advantage. Guerrillas know that language is a powerful weapon, when used well. The following chapter introduces a set of linguistic skills to compliment what you've read already.

CHAPTER 3

Language as a Tool

S O FAR I HAVE shown that words are tools that act as a catalyst in the process of motivation; they are not the means of motivation. The means is appealing to the unconscious mind, through subtle messages that permit the prospect's mind to build associations without direct instruction. It must also be acknowledged that language is an incredibly powerful tool when used properly in a focused manner and in the desired context.

In Chapter 2 I discussed the three primary communicative channels – visual, auditory and kinesthetic. I briefly touched on how language can pace and lead anyone from one state (even their preferred state) to another. Here I present methods and strategies that will add to that arsenal of weapons. You will be given an insight into some of the most persuasive tools available in modern-day marketing. The goal? Precision persuasion for profit.

This chapter details many of the language models first identified by Bandler and Grinder for therapy and commercial use when constructing their NLP model, called the Meta Model. I've said this already, but please be very clear – this book is not an NLP book. There are many great NLP books available already, and some excellent NLP training courses are easily accessible to all. This book is not a competitive product. Guerrilla Marketing has embraced many of the patterns and structures offered by NLP and married them with the time-proven marketing principles that are the foundation of Guerrilla Marketing. The goal of this chapter is not to teach you NLP, but to enable you to understand how language patterns identified within NLP (and specifically the Milton Model) have been included within modern Guerrilla Marketing strategies, and can be applied to your marketing today.

The Meta and Milton Models

This book refers to two linguistic models:

1. The Meta Model
2. The Milton Model

The Meta Model

This refers to a model developed by the creators of NLP (Dr Richard Bandler and John Grinder.) The model provides questions that eliminate ambiguity through deletion, distortion and generalisation. The goal of the Meta Model is therefore to provide an enquiry system to absolutely identify each and every part of a sentence structure, and thus specify experience more fully.

The Milton Model

The late Dr Milton Erickson is considered to have been one of the greatest therapists in American history. Bandler and Grinder modelled his hypnotic language patterns, and named the model after him. The Milton Model is the opposite of the Meta Model, in that it provides the user with ways of being artfully vague. This permits a communicator to make statements that sound specific, and yet are vague enough that the listener or reader must fill in the gaps from their own personal experiences. This is an incredibly powerful weapon for Guerrilla Marketers.

Highlighted here are four basic language patterns from the Milton Model that can be easily applied to your everyday Guerrilla Marketing campaigns:

1. Presupposition

2. Deletion

3. Ambiguity

4. Embedded Commands

Each of these patterns is packed full of Guerrilla value and can prove priceless when used correctly, and worthless when used improperly. Take time to study this chapter. The material is not complex – just probably different from anything you've read before. Stick with it, as there are millions of pounds, dollars, euros and yen buried in this chapter, and it might only require that you act upon one or two of these strategies to release the riches.

Using presuppositions

I've chosen to begin with this language pattern because it is the most powerful of all language patterns. Communication expertise is the single most important skill for any Guerrilla Marketer in modern commerce, and skilfully handling presuppositions is among the most persuasive of abilities.

When using presuppositions, we seek to give the prospect or customer lots of choices, when we have actually managed the offering in such a way that all the choices presuppose the desired response. Artfully manipulative? You bet.

Now, read the statement below and memorise it. Make it your mantra, and if you take nothing else from this book, take this:

Presupposition is the quickest, easiest and most effective means of persuading the unconscious mind, when used by a skilled communicator.

That's the reason you bought this book, right? You seek to influence. Presupposition is the Holy Grail of professional marketers – yet almost none use it skilfully or consistently. Those that do create great marketing campaigns. Those that do not use it well take solace in their few awards won for marketing efforts – even when profits have dived.

Bandler and Grinder identified seven 'presupposition forms' and I strongly feel that Guerrillas need an awareness of all seven forms.

1. Subordinate clauses of time

These clauses use words such as *when, while, as, during, before*, etc.

'When will you be placing the order?' This presupposes that an order will be placed, and instead asks that a decision is made regarding when.

'Would you like a coffee while we finalise this deal?' This directs the listener's attention to the question of coffee or not, and presupposes that the deal will be finalised.

'As you read this book, you'll discover more about our history.' This presupposes that you will read the book, and that you'll make a discovery.

'I'd like to arrange the delivery before you complete the order.' This presupposes that there will be a delivery and you will complete the order.

2. Or

Typically, *or* is used to presuppose that at least one of several alternatives will occur. The bad news is that this is also the most misused of all presuppositions. I'm sure you've been subject to the very obvious close, 'Which is better for you, Monday or Tuesday?' Although this is an example of a presupposition utilising 'or', it is a tired old technique that has been presented in almost every sales and marketing book in history. As such, it is hardly cutting edge.

Frankly, it should not be used as a close. It is a more powerful tool if used as a soft step.

'**Would you rather take delivery before or after your factory shutdown?**' This presupposes that you will take delivery and have a factory shutdown – the only question is in what order.

3. Ordinal numerals

These are words such as *first, second, another*, etc. The most effective use for this type of pattern is to presuppose more than one action or occurrence, and use the form to indicate order.

'**You've probably decided which of the two units you want delivered first.**' This presupposes that the two units will be delivered – the only question is which will be first.

'**You may wonder which campaign will gain market share first.**' This presupposes that both campaigns will gain market share – the question is which will be the first to do so. If you used this pattern with a client, they would simply accept that the presupposition is true, providing you had built rapport first. So although you have not directly said that both campaigns will gain market share, their unconscious mind accepts it as true.

4. Awareness predicates

These include such words as *realise, notice* and *know*. These are usually placed early in a sentence, and the result is that everything after that insertion is presupposed. Then the only question is whether the listener is aware of the point you're making.

'**Have you noticed that we've almost closed this deal?**' This presupposes that the deal is almost closed. The question is whether the listener is aware of the fact.

Other examples include:

'**Do you realise that we are the market leader?**'

'Have you noticed how consistent our quality is?'

'Do you know that ordering this week will gain you a 5 per cent discount?'

5. Change of time verbs and adverbs

These are words such as *continue, still, already, begin, stop*, etc.

'I'm sure you'll continue to enjoy our high-quality materials.' This presupposes that you are already enjoying the high-quality materials.

'So you're still interested in a trial of our new range?' This presupposes that you were interested in the trial in the past.

'I'm certain you've noticed the advances we have already made.' This presupposes that the advances have been made before now.

6. Adverbs and adjectives

These are very often, although not always, words that end in 'ly'. In hypnosis, these words are often slipped into an induction as the 'ly' suffix permits their stealth positioning. Examples are *easily, slowly, deeply*, etc.

'How quickly can you arrange the meeting?' This presupposes that the meeting can be arranged; the only question is how quickly it can be arranged.

'Do you agree we are slowly progressing?' This presupposes that we are progressing; the question is at what speed.

'Are you fully committed to this project?' This presupposes that you are committed to the project, and only asks how fully.

7. Commentary adjectives and adverbs

These are words such as *fortunately, luckily, happily*, etc. Typically, everything after this type of word is presupposed.

'**Fortunately, the problems we've had in the past have now been addressed, and corrected.**' This presupposes everything after the first word.

Learning to use these patterns is not difficult. Spend some time developing your own, based on the examples you've just seen. Make a list of sentences that you feel comfortable using, and start to practise their delivery.

Combining presuppositions

A brilliant method of increasing the power of presuppositions is to assemble a small group of them in a sentence. Guerrillas know that the more that is presupposed in a sentence, the more difficult it is for the listener to unravel the total sentence and question any one presupposition. For example:

'**I don't know how soon you'll notice that we've increased your efficiency and profitability, because the advances that we've already made will make you wonder which has had the most effect.**'

This sentence presupposes that:

1. There are increases in efficiency and profitability.

2. We're responsible for the increases.

3. You will notice the increases; the question is 'When?'

4. Advances have already been made.

5. We're responsible for those advances.

6. Increases have had an effect upon something or someone.

7. Advances will cause you to wonder about the effects.

If you can learn to build sentence structures like this, very soon you'll begin to see that your persuasive abilities are rapidly improving. It is not complicated. You just need to be clear about your goals before you open your mouth. Before you say a single word, consider what you are trying to accomplish with that utterance. What would you like to presuppose when speaking to a prospect that is close to signing the deal? What do you need them to assume is true? Have you noticed yet that this whole book is packed full of presuppositions? (There's another one – an awareness predicate used to presuppose that this book is packed full of presuppositions. The question is not if the presuppositions are there, just whether or not you have noticed them yet.)

The first time you intentionally use presuppositions and get a positive response from a prospect or client, you'll begin to grin. It may start as a wry smile, a warm tingle or some other sensation, but soon you will remember my words here – and you will grin, safe in the knowledge that you've discovered the power of presupposition.

Using deletion

This language pattern is slightly more complex than presuppositions, but once understood is an asset to any Guerrilla. Deletion is where a major noun phrase is completely missing from the sentence. In Guerrilla Marketing we need to be aware of deletion, as if it is not monitored carefully it can ruin a campaign or message by permitting an unintended derivation – resulting in miscommunication, as illustrated by the following examples:

'**My boss was angry.**' Your boss was angry about something, but this sentence does not explain about what.

'**I have a problem.**' You have a problem with something or someone, but this sentence does not explain what or who the problem is.

'**You must be excited!**' The person must be excited about something, but this sentence doesn't detail the source of excitement.

Now to understand the potential issues with using deletion, consider this sentence:

'Guerrilla Marketing International placed the advert.' This sentence is essentially a complete representation of the deep structure, and thus the intended communication, that is a noun called 'Guerrilla Marketing International' performed the action of 'placing' another noun called 'advert'.

However, now consider this sentence:

'The advert was placed.' There is clearly a deletion, as we now no longer know who or what placed the advert. This is an incomplete representation of the deep structure.

Many marketing executives unintentionally present marketing messages full of deletion. Guerrillas know that this can prove fatal, as each and every recipient of a message will have their own history, experience and background to call upon to enable an understanding of the incomplete deep structure.

When creating marketing messages and developing copy, however, you must consider using deletion, as it does have its place in modern marketing. If used in an expert manner, deletion can capture the imagination of each and every recipient of the intended message. Consider this: when you present a sentence utilising deletion, the recipient is required to complete the derivation of the message by examining their past, their beliefs and their understanding of their own model of the world. So what if you could create excitement, pleasure and bliss by using deletion? Wouldn't that be powerful marketing?

'Purchasing can be easy for you.' Who's purchasing and purchasing what?

'The amazing prices excite us!' Who is amazed by the prices?

'This service offering is thrilling!' Thrilling to whom?

'We know exactly how you feel.' Feel about what or whom?

'You can buy this entertaining package.' To whom is the package entertaining?

Each of these sentences is a positive use of deletion, as they require that the recipient create their own understanding of the marketing message. If positioned properly and supported by copy that creates rapport and maintains congruency with the overall marketing message, deletion used in this way provides results that are by and large positive. Never forget, prospects and customers are not robots.

Using ambiguity

This is an important tool that is used to create mild confusion or disorientation, which can be very useful in the preparation for a delivery of an embedded command structure, which we discuss later in this chapter (see page 45). Ambiguity also requires that the listener actively participate in creating the meaning of a message. In all marketing, interaction is key – and ambiguity absolutely necessitates that interaction, or the listener will not understand.

Within the Milton Model, four types of ambiguity have been classified, but for the purposes of this book only one type is discussed – scope ambiguities. (As already explained, this book is not intended to be an NLP book. Although the four types of ambiguity each have their place and function, three of them are better suited to therapy, hypnosis and personal development than they are to Guerrilla Marketing; as the evolution of Guerrilla Marketing continues, it may well be that we will soon accept even more of the NLP model into our material.)

A 'scope ambiguity' occurs where it is unclear how much of the sentence a verb, adverb or adjective applies to. For example:

'Click here for your free ebook and software.' This could mean that you click here for your free ebook and software (which you may or may not have to pay for), or that you click here for your free ebook and free software.

Each of the following sentences offers a scope ambiguity too:

'**Soon you'll realise that we've won the deal and the work will begin.**' In this example, it is unclear whether the term 'realise' refers to the whole sentence or just the winning of the deal.

'**As you read this document you'll begin to appreciate that we're leading the market and your company can benefit from our expertise.**' Here it is unclear whether the verb 'appreciate' refers to the whole sentence or only everything before the word 'and'.

'**Call now to book your free conference seat and consultancy session.**' This is not necessarily a good language pattern to use, but you will see it used a lot. It is unclear whether the consultancy session is free too, or only the conference seat. The issue with this type of pattern is that it raises the expectation of the prospect, who upon calling you is then disappointed to find that the consultancy is not free. Guerrillas know that false promises are not good marketing.

'**As you read this letter you'll slowly begin to accept our pedigree and unique marketing skills.**' In this example, it is unclear whether you are asking the prospect to 'accept' your pedigree and unique marketing skills, or just your pedigree.

When used alongside presuppositions, deletion and embedded commands, this type of structure can be very persuasive. Persuasion requires that you have the prospect's attention, have a level of rapport and present suggestion at the unconscious level.

Using embedded commands

The three language patterns detailed thus far will enable you to present a suggestion in a very persuasive manner, and this one will really hammer your message home.

Right from the offset you need to understand that embedded commands do not work well unless you have the prospect's attention and have built rapport. When we introduce this language pattern during our training courses, everyone immediately sees the power of embedded commands. The more difficult part of the training involves learning how to capture the prospect's attention, and build rapport.

In later chapters we introduce methods to capture attention, so at this point let's look at building rapport.

Typically, building rapport is a personal, face-to-face action. There are many books that introduce methods including advanced body language, matching preferred communication channels, and using hypnotic language and other non-verbal behaviours to build trust. However, in marketing we rarely have the luxury of meeting our prospects, so we need something else. The Guerrilla's first-choice weapon is 'undeniable truth statements'.

Traditional sales and marketing has always subscribed to the belief that the more 'yes' responses you get from a prospect, the closer to the purchase you become. Well here's a newsflash – *this is not the case*.

To move a prospect from total apathy to a purchasing decision requires rapport to be built and the prospect to trust you. To build rapport, the prospect needs to feel that there is a state of agreement between you, not necessarily that they feel the need to keep saying 'yes'. A simple means of building that state of agreement is to offer undeniable truth statements.

Within Sun Tzu's *The Art of War* (see Resources, page 170) it is written: 'Where there is agreement, there can be no battle. An adversary may only exist as an adversary should you permit it.' The relevance of this statement to Guerrilla marketers lies in the understanding that rapport is a natural state, and is usually damaged by your own poor communication. If there is a state of agreement between you and your prospects, they are moving towards the purchasing decision.

Guerrillas present undeniable truth statements to build rapport quickly. After all, if the statements are undeniably true, how can the prospect not agree? Thus the state of agreement is formed, even if the responses have been 'no'.

So how can rapport be built, with a string of 'no' responses, flying in the face of traditional teaching? Consider these questions:

'You don't have problems with delivery, do you?'

'You wouldn't expect to accept financial losses, would you?'

'You wouldn't object to considering partnerships, would you?'

Each of these questions builds rapport, despite obtaining a 'no' response. How? The questions are presented in such a way as to show understanding, and thus creating a state of agreement. The key therefore lies in questions that *show an understanding*.

By demonstrating an understanding, rapport is developed at an increased rate. As humans, we naturally seek out (and are most comfortable with) people that we consider to be like ourselves. That is the reason why we have clubs and associations. Stamp collectors like to be around other stamp collectors. Motor sport fans enjoy the company of other motor sport fans. These people enjoy each other's company because they have very apparent shared interests. In the same way, your prospects will feel most comfortable around people who display an understanding of their business.

I've already introduced undeniable truth statements as a means of building rapport quickly, and you now know that you don't need a string of 'yes' responses to build rapport (despite the contents of almost every sales and marketing training course available, outside of Guerrilla Marketing). With these essential pieces of information in hand, we can now develop a strategy for preparing to use embedded commands.

Undeniable truth statements are very easy to create. You simply make a statement that is true, beyond all argument or conjecture. Examples could be:

'We are sitting here.'

'This is our first meeting.'

'I contacted you.'

'Our companies have never worked together before now.'

'You have seen our products.'

'It's raining outside.'

'It is now May.'

Each and every one of these statements is undeniably true, and as such builds rapport. Marry these statements with questions that display an understanding of your prospects' business and you will find that you are building a state of agreement, which is particularly conducive to the presentation of embedded commands.

Before we actually construct the embedded command, let's go over the prerequisites:

1. Get their attention.

2. Use questions to *clearly* display understanding.

3. Present undeniable truth statements.

4. Ensure a solid state of agreement.

When, and only when, these factors have been satisfied should you consider using embedded commands.

So what exactly is an embedded command? This is a language pattern where rather than giving a command directly, it is embedded within a larger sentence structure, often covertly. The result is that the command is understood and accepted by the unconscious mind, and possibly unnoticed by the conscious mind.

We know that rapid access of the unconscious mind can be accomplished by using the term 'you' or by using the name of the listener. How many times have you heard your own name, and turned to respond without thinking? This is an unconscious action. When you hear your name, your brain assumes there is some interest for you, and creates an unconscious response. So, to embed a command, we usually use either a name, or the term 'you' to access the unconscious mind, then follow that with a command. In each of these examples the embedded command is in italics.

'I'd like to have you *give me a call.*'

'I don't know how soon you *will place the order.*'

'It's OK if you *want to visit our website.*'

Earlier on (see page 7) I explained that the unconscious mind doesn't understand negation. Here again I put this knowledge to good use. Consider the sentence:

'I know you want to visit our website.'

Although this sentence contains an embedded command, the directive is not at all subtle or covert. In some cases this would work, as there is always a place for a steamroller! However, in many cases the conscious recognition of this directive will result in a polarity response, that is in a refusal to accept the directive. Using our understanding of the unconscious mind and negation, a better option would be:

'I don't know if you want to visit our website.'

This is a softer, less obvious, yet equally powerful means of embedding the same command. In the huge majority of instances, the more subtle version will be better received. Remember the blue elephant (see page 6)? The command I gave you was, 'Don't think of a blue elephant.' Had I given you the more direct command, 'Think of a blue elephant now,' your brain may well have still created the image, but would you have felt that it was formed freely, or would you have felt violated and controlled? Do you want to take that risk with your prospects and customers?

To allow the delivery of an embedded command to become even more subtle, Guerrillas often spread the command across two sentences:

'I don't know if you *want to visit our website. Now,* if you do then we have some great offers.'

Did you spot the full extent of the embedded command?

By simply marking the command in italics (a technique detailed later, see page 89) and including the first part of the second sentence, we added a time reference to the command. So the embedded command now reads, 'want to visit our website now'.

Adding a time reference can improve the performance of an embedded command six or seven fold. To make the construction of similar commands easier, Guerrillas use this method:

1. Divide a page into four sections.

Section 1

want to visit our website

can call me

will book an appointment

Section 2

now

soon

today

Section 3

           want to visit our website. Now,

                  can call me. Today,

Section 4

I don't know if you want to visit our website. Now, if you do then you'll see our client list.

I'm not sure if you can call me. Today, I'm in the office until 6 p.m.

2. Select and list the desired commands in Section 1, for example *want to visit our website, can call me, will book an appointment,* etc.

3. Select and list some time references, but only use references that can be used to start a sentence, and place them in Section 2, for example *now, tomorrow, today, soon,* etc.

4. Take one item from Section 1 and one item from Section 2 and place them together in Section 3 with a full stop between them and a comma after the time reference.

5. Take the language structure from Section 3 and place it in Section 4, then add copy before and after the structure, ensuring that it makes good grammatical sense.

For increased persuasive power, I personally like to stack two or three embedded commands in linking sentences, for example:

'I don't know if you want to work with us. Now, it would be cheeky of me to claim you should work with us. Today, I can tell you that companies who do work with us become rapidly profitable.'

Do you recognise the two commands?

Stacking language patterns is not a technique limited to embedded commands. (Remember the example I gave you in the presuppositions section, see page 37?) Precision persuasion of the unconscious mind is accomplished more quickly and easily the more of these language patterns you use. Furthermore, if you stack multiple patterns together, very often the unconscious mind doesn't spend too much of its precious resources interpreting the data, preferring to identify patterns and seek out congruence. (At its most basic level, congruence means maintaining a consistent and predictable identity in everything that you do. It is discussed in detail on page 139.)

Guerrilla Marketing has always sought to utilise the most advanced methods and strategies available, and the material in this chapter is cutting edge. Use the examples provided here to model your own strategies. Learn how to use these patterns, and practise them. The more expert you become in their everyday use, the more persuasive you will become.

Precision Persuasion

THIS CHAPTER WILL SHOCK you as it flies in the face of anything you've read before. Let me start with a myth that is to be found in modern sales and marketing, and has gained momentum outside of Guerrilla Marketing. Too many people have been beaten into submission and accepted this myth as true. Don't be one of them.

Using 'pain' in traditional sales and marketing methods

Traditional sales and marketing says that the easiest and quickest method for moving a prospect from total apathy to the purchasing decision is to identify a pain, build upon and expand that pain, then offer a solution. An example might be along these lines:

Bob: So, Mr Client, you say your delivery is slower than that of your competition?

Client: Yes, Bob. We take seven to ten days while our competition takes five to seven days.

Bob: And you've lost business because of this?

Client: Yes, probably three or four customers last month.

Bob: You said earlier that your average order is about £10,000. So you're losing up to £40,000 a month?

Client: That's about right, I suppose.

Bob: That's equal to £480,000 a year! Your management must be livid. Is it demoralising for your staff?

Client: Of course. We may have to downsize if we can't find a solution.

Bob: So there is a genuine concern that jobs may go?

Client: Yes, it's a very real possibility.

Bob: It may not be necessary, let me show you what we're proposing.

For decades this has been accepted as the leading, if not only, method worthy of consideration by sales and marketing professionals worldwide. I have news for you: it's not the best or most effective method any more. Welcome to modern Guerrilla Marketing!

The traditional method that I've just described requires that three things happen:

1. The prospect is forced to consider a situation that is unpleasant by its very nature. The result is that the strategy actually makes the prospect feel bad.

2. The prospect's unpleasant feeling is then built up, expanded upon and amplified.

3. Finally, a solution is offered to reduce or remove 'the pain'.

So my question to you is this: do you believe that you need to make your prospects feel bad before they will buy from you? I don't believe this to be the case.

If you wanted to have a relationship with someone and that person was single but resisted, would you worry that person with stories about people being alone? If the resistance continued, would you continue the stories by describing how burglars target single homeowners? Would you continue the barrage of negative information until that person submitted and agreed to a relationship with you? How strong do you think that relationship would be, when the person was with you only through fear? This is the way traditional sales and marketing work.

Traditional marketers may tell you that identifying the pain and then offering a solution is a great way to build rapport, as the prospect will see you as having an interest in their affairs, and the fact that you have offered a solution that makes their life easier will establish the foundations upon which a strong relationship can be built. Let me tell you, this is simply not true.

Offering positive solutions

It is essential to your future success that you fully comprehend these next two sentences:

Identifying a pain, expanding on the pain, and then offering a solution is not good marketing. There is an easier, more efficient and more responsible way.

Modern Guerrilla Marketing has recognised a method that builds stronger relationships, removes the risk of buyer's remorse (see page 27) and ensures that the client is always happy with their purchase. When clients are happy with their purchases, they are more likely to provide testimonials and referrals than at any other time – and these are the bread and butter of all Guerrillas.

There is no magic to this massively profitable formula. It is a method that is used by elite therapists across the world. Consider my last statement carefully. There are many competent and successful therapists, but there are very few elite therapists. In the same way, elite Guerrilla Marketers recognise this formula as the way forward, throughout the evolution of Guerrilla Marketing. I'll make this as simple as possible, to ensure complete comprehension for all:

Offer a better choice.

So simple it's hard to believe it works? Well, it does.

Forget identifying pains. Your prospects know what their problems are. They don't need you, or indeed want you, to identify their pains. They definitely don't want to talk about them. They want to know what you can do to make their lives better.

If you need to resort to identifying pains to sell your product or service, you must ask yourself whether what you are offering is exciting enough. If your offering is not exciting, make it so. Using traditional 'pains' sales and marketing techniques is a substitute for developing great ideas. If you spend the same amount of time and effort on making your offering exciting that you already spend in identifying pains, you'll make more profit.

The 'pains' method is little more than a polished way of saying, 'If you don't buy this, your work life will be miserable forever.' That isn't a great way to forge a relationship. Giving prospects and customers a better choice, on the other hand, will make them feel great – and you should aim to present your offering in such a way that after the purchase, every time your customer looks at what they have bought, it will make them feel great again.

Your goal should always be to create excitement and make your prospects or customers feel great. In the example of a conversation between Bob and Mr Client (see page 53), Bob was trying to do the opposite, as his strategy focused on the ability to 'save' Mr Client from his 'pain'. If a Guerrilla Marketer (we'll call him Mike) had been using the 'better choice' strategy, the conversation may have looked more like this:

Mike: So, Mr Client, you say your delivery is slower than that of your competition?

Client: Yes, Mike. We take seven to ten days and our competition is about five to seven days.

Mike: And how much quicker would you like to see your delivery?

Client: If we could get it down to five to seven days that would be great.

Mike: OK, so five to seven days would be great. What about if we could get you down to three to four days?

Client: That would be incredible!

Mike: Would that make your life easier?

Client: Oh, yes! The whole department would benefit.

Mike: Just so I understand; if we could get your delivery down to three to four days you say it would be incredible, would make your life easier and benefit the whole department?

Client: That's exactly right!

Mike: Then I'm about to make you a very happy man! Let me show you what we're proposing.

In this example Mike is focused throughout on building positive feelings about the possibilities available to the client. By concentrating on positive outcomes, the client becomes excited internally. Excitement is an important part of any motivation strategy, and a wonderful feeling to instil in anyone.

Notice that Mike did not, at any point, describe anything negative or create any images that could be interpreted as negative. Guerrillas know that excellent questioning skills are key to communications expertise. Mike only ever posed questions that created positive images about the future. Presenting questions in this manner is a skill that should be practised. Whenever a prospect or customer offers a statement that could lead down a negative route, present a question that requires the listener to consider a positive outcome.

1. Client: We have a real brand image problem at the moment.

You: How would you like to see your brand portrayed?

2. Client: We lost 5 per cent market share in the last quarter.

You: How will your Board respond when you win that 5 per cent back?

3. Client: We have a staff retention problem.

You: How will it feel when you have a settled and successful team?

4. Client: Our last marketing campaign made a loss.

You: Who will be credited with the success of this next campaign?

5. Client: Our competitors are advancing more quickly than we are.

You: How will you measure your success when you surpass them?

Each of these questions requires that the client consider a positive outcome. A prospect or client in a positive state of mind is more motivated to purchase than someone who is buying through aversion to 'pain' – despite what traditional marketers may tell you.

When someone visualises a positive outcome, their brain creates large amounts of pleasure drugs, including serotonin. A brain that has plentiful amounts of pleasure drugs in circulation operates more efficiently than one that doesn't, and therefore permits better information retention. So prospects and customers will remember not only more about the product or service you are offering, but also the associations that they create between your offering and how they feel. If they create pleasant (or even delightful) associations with your products, services and indeed with you, that can't hurt your business relationship, can it?

On the other hand, a customer who bought to avoid a 'pain' would always carry an unconscious feeling that they were forced to make that purchase, and will never be truly loyal. Satisfied customers are easy to find, but loyal customers are rare. As a Guerrilla, your goal is to gain a throng of loyal customers. The way to build this mass of loyal customers is to give your prospects a better choice.

I recently hosted some training for a prestige car dealership. The staff at this dealership had received sales training in the past, and the strategies presented to them had been completely pain based.

It's amazed me for years that prestige car sales closure rates are not higher. Think about it. A prospect takes the time and effort to travel to a dealership, knowing that the dealership specialises in high-quality, high-priced vehicles. The expectation is high price. The fact that the prospect walks through the door means that you should be able to sell them a car.

Until I introduced Guerrilla Marketing, the sales team would typically approach the prospect, ask some questions to identify the prospect's needs, then proceed to explain why other cars were inferior in build quality, could be uncomfortable on long journeys and could even risk life in an accident. The prospect was therefore not really in the most positive of states.

Moreover, using 'pains' methods in this way can be dangerous. The chances are that the prospect chose their last car assuming that it was the best choice available at the budget assigned. If you then tell that prospect that any car other than yours is a bad choice, you will shatter any rapport you have made with them. Who likes to be told they made a bad decision?

It was clear that visitors to the dealership needed to be given a better choice.

I created a set of scripts, each short and succinct. The opening two sentences for each script were the same:

Do you want a car that will make you feel wonderful?

Do you deserve to feel great every time you look at it, knowing what you've accomplished in getting this car today?

It wasn't complicated. It wasn't difficult. I simply offered a better choice. Stop and think about it. The first question was, 'Do you want a car that will make you feel wonderful?' It's a rhetorical question. I don't know anyone who would answer, 'No, thank you. I'd like a car that depresses me. I was hoping to suffer buyer's remorse for the next three to five years!' When someone seeks to buy a new vehicle, they are excited. The challenge is to harness that excitement and motivation, build a visualisation of a positive outcome and position the offering in such a way as to show the prospect that they will feel great about the decision.

Now consider the second sentence and ask yourself whether you can honestly think of anyone who would say, 'No, I just want a car that makes me feel worthless every time I look at it.' Your goal as a Guerrilla is to build bliss into every purchasing decision that is made by your prospects and customers. Whether your customers buy professional services, cars, property, computers or anything else at all, after the purchase, every single time they look at their purchase they should feel that it was a great decision, because it makes them feel great. Remember, you are selling feelings.

Once the staff at the dealership recognised this, they began to use language that created positive visual imagery. Customers were excited about buying the cars, and they were excited about the fact that every time they drove the cars they would feel wonderful. The results were a clear indicator for all – the dealership staff sold more vehicles in one month than they had in the previous four.

People want to feel good about themselves, and about the decisions they make. If you can build that into your marketing you will see your profits soar. Using identified pains to make people feel bad about their present positions, and then offering solutions to ease that pain, does not make people feel good about themselves. People in a negative state make bad decisions. We all know people who bounce from one bad relationship to another. Why? Because they make relationship decisions when they're in a bad state. The same is often true of people with financial difficulties. Many people find themselves in a downwards spiral of debt because they make decisions about their financial future when they are in a bad state.

I've said this before and I'll say it again now; your body can only do what your brain tells it to do. You can control your own mind. You can help others control theirs. Build positive states in others and watch the changes that occur.

If you honestly believe that bad things will happen, they usually will because your actions (defined by your unconscious mind, based on your beliefs) will exhibit behaviours that support your beliefs. The good news is that the reverse is also true; if you build beliefs that good things will happen, your brain will ensure that your behaviours support these beliefs.

Guerrillas know that if you create positive states in prospects and customers, and then provide information and other soft steps that build a belief that your product or service will ensure that wonderful feelings are coming their way, they will commit to the purchase *much* quicker.

Overcoming objections

The next strategy that you need to be introduced to is one that all business professionals have to be familiar with. All sales and marketing professionals know that they will definitely encounter objections from prospects and customers. Usually, the same objections occur over and over again. My question to you is this: do you use the traditional method, whereby you have rehearsed responses to 'overcome' objections, or do you apply a modern Guerrilla Marketing strategy?

Let's start with the idea of 'overcoming' objections. According to the *Concise Oxford English Dictionary*, to overcome is 'to defeat or succeed in controlling something'. So, in essence, to overcome an objection, you must defeat it or control it. Traditional sales and marketing advocates the former, Guerrilla Marketing the latter.

In order to defeat an objection, you must convince the prospect that their objection is flawed in some way. To suggest to a prospect that their reality is wrong is a dangerous game. (What if their blue elephant is bigger than yours, and has had Kung Fu training, or is familiar with small arms weapons or drives a tank?) Telling a prospect that they are wrong does not build rapport, and prospects rarely buy from people with whom they do not share a state of rapport.

That aside, defeating an objection requires that you assume an adversarial position with your prospect. This in itself is not always a bad thing, and indeed many Guerrilla Marketing strategies assume this mind-set. However, by trying to defeat an objection, you are in effect saying to your prospect, 'You are wrong. I know better than you, so accept my view as true.' This is not precision persuasion.

Guerrilla Marketing is always aware of the power of language, and accepts that objections are a component part of the sales and marketing process. With this in mind, there are two strategies I want to offer you now:

1. Powerful questions.

2. Inoculating against objections.

Powerful Questions

Your ability to construct questions in a manner that actually achieves the desired goal will eventually define your success or failure. The first skill that you definitely must master is the creation of open questions. An open question is one that cannot be answered 'yes' or 'no' – this type is called a closed question. Open questions require that the reader or listener go through a derivation process to develop an understanding, and thus an answer. For example, a closed question might be:

Can you create more profit from your existing clients?

Whereas posing the same question as an open question could be:

How can you create more profit from your existing clients?

In the closed question above, the reader can spend a minimal amount of resource to come to an answer, or can simply answer without calculating an answer. Furthermore, if the answer given is 'no' then the conversation is to all intents and purposes over. However, in the open version of the same question the reader unquestionably must go through a derivation of their experiences and understanding of the question to give an answer. In the example above, the reader has to go inside and create a visualisation of how they can create more profit from existing clients. This is interaction. When constructing questions Guerrillas always seek this interaction, with one exception. It is OK to use a closed question when you are absolutely certain of the response – as in the case of the questions created for the car dealership (see page 58).

The second question construction skill that you need to master is the ability to turn an objection into a question. At the most basic level, objections cannot be 'overcome' without one party giving ground. As such, it would appear that an objection cannot be answered in a manner that is not adversarial. This is not true. If you can turn an objection into a question, you can answer that question. So, when a prospect offers an objection, repeat the objection back to the prospect in the form of a question. For example:

1. Client: We think your prices are too high, compared to those of your competitors.

You: So you're asking why our prices are higher than our competition?

2. Client: I'm not happy with your delivery taking so long.

You: So you're asking why our delivery takes so long?

3. Client: We have a problem with the additional service charges.

You: So you're asking why we charge the additional fees?

In each of the above examples, if the question offered by you is confirmed as true, then you can answer it. When you have given your answer, simply ask, 'Does that answer your question?' This presupposes that it was a question and not an objection, and (as a closed question) requires either a 'yes' or a 'no'. If the answer is 'no' then a period of silence on your part will cause the prospect to feel the need to qualify the 'no'.

Inoculating against objections

If we are going to travel somewhere where we know there is a risk of illness, we can inoculate against that illness. If we know that a particular disease is established in any place, we can inoculate against that disease. Dr Richard Bandler asked the brilliant question, 'Why not inoculate against objections?' and frankly I could not think of any good reason – so Guerrilla Marketing embraced the method.

If you truly know your industry, your clients, your prospects and your own offering, you should be able to accurately predict which objections are most frequently offered. If you know which objections are likely to be thrown your way, why not prepare for them by preventing them in the first instance?

One of my clients offers an excellent web design service. Their portfolio is impressive and their prices reflect this. They offer a premium product for a premium price. They asked me to address an issue that kept rearing its ugly head. They would approach an organisation and offer a web design service. All would go well until the potential client would complete their collection of competitive quotes, realise that my client was one of the most expensive and offer the contract to another bidder.

As account after account slipped through their fingers, we decided to try an inoculation strategy. We agreed that when presenting their prices, my client would direct the conversation:

My client: So now you have our proposal document, how will you manage the decision-making process?

End user: We will put together a spreadsheet and list all the features and benefits of each proposal.

My client: Then perhaps we should withdraw our proposal now.

End user: Why?

My client: I've enjoyed working with you, and believe we could have a long business relationship. We don't want to waste your time, or our own. When you put together the spreadsheet and review our portfolio, our benefits will clearly exceed the competition's and you'll feel that we're your first choice. Then one of your colleagues will point out that we are one of the most expensive and will try to pressure you to accept an inferior proposal based on price alone. I don't want you to be responsible for accepting an inferior proposal because of your budget. So maybe we should just withdraw our proposal now.

End user: No, you don't need to do that. I'm managing the decision.

My client: But what will you tell your colleagues about the price issue?

End user: I'll tell them that your portfolio shows that you have the expertise we need and it's worth paying that little bit more.

My client: If you're sure you can do that, we'd love to work with you.

In this example, my client actually had the end user qualify his own reasons for purchasing. By going through this process, my client inoculated against the price objection. Having qualified his own reasons for rejecting the price objection, the end user could never offer that objection to my client.

Isn't that beautifully simple? It works for any industry and any product or service. Providing you know which objections are likely to arise, you can inoculate against them.

Creating and delivering an inoculation against an objection is a simple process:

1. Identify the most frequently offered objections.

2. Determine how to best position your offering, when considering the validity of the objection.

3. Create a presentation that accepts that the objection exists, but is not necessarily relevant.

4. Have the purchaser confirm their acceptance of your position and ask the purchaser to qualify their position.

Good examples of inoculations are:

- 'In the past, when our clients haven't completed a proper cost of ownership model, they've suggested that our prices are too high. However, when they finally do complete the model, they realise the error in their initial beliefs.' This inoculates against the 'your prices are too high' objection.

- 'I have had inexperienced purchasing staff complain about our service charges, but when they complete proper due diligence they see that our service charges actually save them money.' This inoculates against the 'your service charges are too high' objection.

- 'I sold one of our systems to a purchasing manager in London, and from day one he was whining and moaning about our installation costs. When his staff calculated the savings he effected by not using his own staff resources, he apologised to me!' This inoculates against the 'your installation costs are high' objection.

When you marry the inoculation strategy with powerful questions, you suddenly have two hugely powerful weapons to add to your arsenal. Add the 'better choice' strategy and you have the most devastating arsenal you've ever had.

The following chapters introduce even more weapons, combinations, methods and strategies that will skyrocket your profits. Enjoy the revolution.

New Guerrilla Marketing Memory Strategy

G UERRILLAS ARE CONSTANTLY looking to develop new marketing weapons, methods and strategies. As Guerrilla Marketing evolves, we are finding new ways of approaching existing tasks in more efficient ways. You are about to learn one of the most important discoveries that we have made. This will make your marketing more effective and even more profitable, and your prospects will be motivated to move to their purchasing decisions quicker.

Repetition as a marketing weapon

Guerrilla Marketing has always championed repetition as the best means of penetrating a prospect's mind. A study was conducted to see how many times you must penetrate a person's mind with your selling proposition before you convert that person from a state of total apathy to a state of purchase readiness. Amazingly, the researchers came up with an answer – nine. Your marketing message must penetrate a prospect's mind nine times before that person will purchase your product or service. Unfortunately, for every three times you present your marketing message, your prospect is paying attention only once.

So, you market by advertising, email, telemarketing, signs, direct mail, anything – and you present your message three times, and it penetrates your prospect's mind one time. What response do you think you get? None. Nothing at all. This is where many marketers stop their activity. Surely if you've presented your marketing message three times, you should have had some response, right? No, absolutely not. As a Guerrilla, you know that patience is the most important Guerrilla trait, and you present your message again. You've now presented your message six times, and penetrated your prospect's mind twice. What happens then? Still nothing.

All right, you present your marketing message nine times, and penetrate your prospect's mind three times. What happens now? Your prospect knows that they have heard of you before – but still no sale. The unconscious mind is well aware of where and when it heard of you, and even remembers your message, but at this point it doesn't feel that the conscious mind needs to know. After all, it's only heard of you three times, and you might be a fly-by-night.

Sticking with the drill, you present your message 12 times and your prospect's mind has been pierced four times. What happens then? The unconscious mind recognises a trend and as a result slowly brings the prospect's conscious awareness into the loop. The prospect realises that they have seen your marketing before, and prompted by the unconscious mind, decides to keep an eye out for your marketing in the future. Remember, prospects require confidence in any organisation from which they are considering purchasing products or services and if they keep seeing your marketing, they assume you must be doing something right. Although the recognition is there after 12 presentations of your message, the sale is not. Still nobody is buying anything.

At the point when you've put out your marketing message 15 times, and your prospect's mind has been accessed five times, the unconscious mind shares its knowledge with the prospect's conscious awareness. The prospect probably reads every word of your advertisement or letter, and maybe even sends away for the brochure that you've been offering since day one.

The Chartered Institute of Purchase and Supply in London researched the longevity of marketing campaigns, and found that 92 per cent of marketing campaigns are significantly altered or halted after 15 presentations. Guerrillas aim to be in the 8 per cent, as although there is still no sale yet, they know that patience is the route to profit.

After you've presented your message 18 times, and you've penetrated a mind six times, that person begins to think of when they'll make the purchase – but still there's no sale yet. Put the word out 21 times and you'll have pierced the prospect's mind seven times. Now the prospect begins to think about what method they will use to pay, and where the money will come from.

Once you've presented your message 24 times, and accessed your prospect's mind eight times, that prospect is pencilling in a specific time and date to make the purchase. Before 'firming up' the purchase time and date, the prospect will speak to friends, colleagues and whomever else they need to consult in order to make the purchase. Finally, you present your marketing message 27 times, and penetrate your prospect's mind nine times, and they buy from you. Eventually the profits come rolling in.

Presenting a marketing message 27 times will take weeks or months. In some industries the purchasing process can take 18 months or more. Guerrillas are patient and are also continually seeking new ways to approach old problems.

Using anchors

I have now identified a means of shortening the purchasing process and reducing the number of marketing message presentations required to reach the buying stage. I am not suggesting that the 27-message method is wrong. I am simply saying that I have improved upon it, as I have isolated a new set of skills that has allowed me to develop a new method. This method has its roots in the award-winning research of a Russian scientist.

Ivan Petrovich Pavlov, born in 1849, spent most of his career studying the mechanisms underlying the digestive system in mammals. He was indeed an accomplished leader in this field, and in 1904 was awarded the Nobel Prize for Physiology. As his work advanced, he began to investigate conditioned reflexes, and many of his discoveries paved the way for the objective science of behaviour.

While working to uncover the secrets of the digestive system, Pavlov also studied what signals triggered related phenomena, such as the secretion of saliva. For example, when a dog encounters food, saliva begins to pour from the salivary glands. Saliva is needed in order to break down certain compounds in food, so the dog's unconscious mind sends the necessary signals to the salivary glands. Pavlov began to investigate further when he saw that dogs he worked with drooled without the proper stimulus. Although no food was in sight, their saliva still dribbled. He eventually discovered that the dogs were reacting to the staff in their laboratory coats. Every time the dogs were served food, the person who served the food was wearing a white laboratory coat. Therefore the dogs reacted as if food was coming every time they saw a white laboratory coat. They had learned to associate white coats with food.

To prove his theory, Pavlov began a series of experiments whereby he struck a bell every time food was served. In a short period of time he only needed to strike the bell for the dogs to respond by salivating, whether food was presented or not. The dogs had learned to associate the sound of the bell with food. In NLP this is referred to as an 'anchor'.

Anchors are one of the most exciting new Guerrilla Marketing weapons, and when used properly can reduce the purchasing process by huge amounts of time, which in turn increases your profits.

An anchor is essentially an internal or external representation that triggers another representation. When it is important to control the content of a representational system, such as a market-ing message, we need a way to ensure access and reaccess to the particular representation associated with that marketing message. This is an anchor.

If you correctly establish an anchor, you no longer need to penetrate your prospect's mind nine times. In fact, if the anchor is associated with an intense representation, you may only need to pierce your prospect's mind once or twice before they make the purchasing decision. Now that is an exciting marketing weapon!

Anchoring is built upon the understanding that when any part of a representation is reintroduced, the other parts of that representation will also be reproduced to some degree. For example, if you can remember a time when you were seriously scared about your own safety, you should be able to recall what you saw. You will probably also be able to remember what you heard and how you felt at that time. You will see what you saw, hear what you heard and feel what you felt. Now, any portion of this representation could be used to access the other parts. If you were asked to recall how you felt, your mind would create an image of the event as well. Since the experience was so highly emotional, you require no repetition of the event, yet you recall it clearly.

If you can create an honest and emotional response in your prospects, you won't need to penetrate their minds nine times. An honest response is one that is created by the unconscious, and not a consciously fashioned response. When a person consciously chooses to respond to a trigger in a certain way, we call that an 'elective response'. This type of response is often driven by peer group pressure, the need to be accepted or simple ego. Some traditional marketing campaigns have used techniques to elicit this type of response, and some have succeeded. However, campaigns that make use of elective responses have short life cycles, as fashions and public opinions change frequently and rapidly. Guerrillas know that the skill is in generating honest responses and establishing anchors while ensuring that the marketing message will be associated with positive or powerful internal states.

Pavlov discovered two ways of creating associations. The first was repetition, the continual association between a stimulus and a response. (This is the principle that Guerrilla Marketing has always championed.) The second was related to linking an intense internal response to a particular stimulus. Both can and should be used.

There are a number of absolutely essential factors that must be considered when establishing anchors.

1. Reinforcement

This is reinforcement of the anchor. When Pavlov was conducting his experiments, he found that if he rang the bell without presenting food to the dogs, the response to the bell would eventually lessen and finally fail.

When the pioneers of email marketing began their campaigns, they made great use of the term 'free' to create a state of excitement. In time, this became an anchor for readers as they trawled through their inboxes. They would see that a subscription, ebook or piece of software was free, and become naturally excited. Soon, though, the anchor had been misused – as 'free' rarely meant free. As a result the majority of people became less responsive to the term, and today the response is weaker than ever before. As was the case with Pavlov's dogs, the anchor had not been accurately and repeatedly reinforced. (It is ironic, but if the term had not been abused, it would be one of the most influential terms on the Internet today.) Guerrillas, conversely, only market something as free when it is genuinely supplied at no cost.

2. Intensity

This is the intensity of the experience that you wish to anchor. The more intense the experience that the individual has at the time the anchor is created, the stronger will be the response when the anchor is reintroduced.

This factor slightly contradicts the previous factor, as we also know that repetition of an anchor is not necessary if the intensity created is very powerful. This is good news for Guerrillas, as it means that anchors can be created very quickly. Just think for a moment – when a person has a phobia about snakes, how many times did they have to be introduced to snakes to become phobic? Usually, it is a single event that may have lasted only a fraction of a second, which embeds the phobia. So now consider this: how many people with a phobia about snakes forget to be scared of snakes? None. Even people with terrible memories never forget to react to their phobia. The intensity of the anchor is such that in a fraction of a second it is so deeply embedded that it instantly brings about a state of phobic reaction every single time the anchor is reintroduced. That is a formidable anchor.

3. Distinctiveness

We already know that anchors are most effective when reinforced, although they can be equally successful with a single presentation, providing the experience is intensely powerful at the time the anchor is created. With this knowledge secured, we can now take into account the third factor for consideration, namely that the more unique the anchor is, the more accurately it will bring about the desired representation – in this case a marketing message.

Guerrillas must at all times remember, however, that as already discussed (see page 9), your prospect's blue elephant will differ from your blue elephant – if you let it. The differences are limited by replicating the reintroduction of the anchor as closely as possible. If you slightly vary the reintroduction, the prospect will begin to add their personal associations to the marketing message that you're trying to communicate.

An excellent example of this very important factor is the 'Marlboro Man'. Over the decades that the marketing campaign was running, his heroic look was never changed. Although originally he was selected to envision a rugged, macho image for Marlboro smokers, it was also recognised by the marketers responsible for the campaign that it was that specific type of cowboy that Marlboro smokers related to. It wasn't just a cowboy smoking that was the anchor. It was a stereotypical cowboy who had been directly associated with 'Marlboro Country'. In all probability, the campaign may not have been so successful if less heroic-looking cowboys had been used to play the part of the Marlboro Man, as then the reintroduction of the anchor would have been somewhat different every time. This in turn would have varied the representation and experience for the prospect.

4. Timing

The fourth component part of the creation of a successful anchor is timing. This is perhaps the most difficult part of the creation process. You absolutely must set the anchor at a time when the intensity of the experience is increasing. In this way, the unconscious mind has a directional trend to follow. If the intensity is escalating, the anchor will be associated with an experience that is also growing. If the timing of the anchor creation is incorrect, that is if it occurs when the most intense part of the state has passed, and the anchor is reintroduced, it will be associated with an experience of decreasing intensity.

Take time to look around you and notice the many anchors that are already in your life. For example, when your partner says, 'I love you,' you get a pleasant feeling inside. This is your brain flooding your system with chemicals that make you feel good. They are called dopamine and serotonin, and are naturally produced in your body and controlled by your unconscious. When someone is told that they are loved, that person can experience a state of euphoria, and possibly a level of nervous tension, too. These feelings are a result of dopamine and serotonin being released, often in conjunction with adrenalin. The unconscious mind associates 'I love you' with this wonderfully emotional response, and anchors it. The result is an anchor that, for many people, lasts a lifetime.

Combining memes with anchors

A meme is a self-explanatory symbol, involving the use of words, action, sounds or images to communicate an entire idea. Australian author Geoff Ayling describes memes as 'operating through the process of chunking complex ideas or concepts down into a simple, easily communicable unit'. Memes are an excellent weapon to employ with anchors. Good examples of memes are:

- The 'Marlboro Man' – instantly presents a rugged, macho, 'man's cigarette' image.

- The 'Slimfast' range of foods – instantly details their use.

- 'Weight Watchers' – instantly details their role.

- 'Michelin Man' – his tyre construction has been in place for decades.

Memes are in fact one of the quickest and easiest devices that can be used to create an anchor. Stop and think about it. If you have a meme that instantly communicates a marketing message, whether it is an image, sound or words, and you can associate that meme with an honest and intense emotional response, isn't that the perfect scenario in which to create an anchor? It certainly is – and you have just uncovered the singularly most powerful marketing combination in Guerrilla Marketing history!

If you can combine a meme with a well-created anchor, you will have an irresistible marketing message. The meme will communicate the desired message, and correct creation of the anchor will ensure that the reintroduction of the meme will bring about an honest and intense emotional response.

The more you experiment with anchors as marketing weapons, the more proficient you will become in their use. Correctly creating, reinforcing and reintroducing anchors are skills that very few marketers possess. When you can accurately and consistently employ anchors, you will begin to see your purchasing cycles reduce, and your other marketing weapons will return profits quicker than you've experienced before.

One excellent example of an anchor in use today is the 'Intel Inside' logo and four-tone jingle. Every single TV or radio advert that mentions Intel *must* display the 'Intel Inside' logo and play the four-tone jingle. It's an absolute requirement that Intel insist upon, and rightly so. The anchor is so well established that in a survey conducted by Guerrilla Marketing UK in 2003, of the sample group surveyed, 88 per cent recognised the four-tone jingle (without visual reference) as belonging to Intel. Why? Because every single time that Intel was mentioned on TV or radio, the four-tone jingle was played. Similarly to Pavlov's dogs, we all learned that the tone had a direct association – and in this case it was with Intel.

Practise using anchors in everyday conversation and in your written marketing too. Soon you will find that using anchors is second nature, and your ability to communicate has been massively enhanced. At the most basic level, marketing is using multiple communication methods to persuade. If your communication skills and tools are more advanced than those of your competitors, then your marketing messages will be better understood and more readily accepted.

Until now, Guerrilla Marketing has offered you repetition as the only means of penetrating a prospect's mind. Anchors are a superb Guerrilla Marketing weapon and enhance your marketing package with advanced psychology. Add anchors to your marketing arsenal today and watch your profits soar.

CHAPTER 6

Writing for the Unconscious Mind

THUS FAR I HAVE presented you with methods and strategies that utilise the written and spoken word. Now it's time to focus specifically on the written word, because the fact is that most marketing is not completed face to face (although the technology to do so is not that far away).

In this chapter I discuss page layout first, as there are many myths surrounding this, and few companies do it well. Next, I introduce some methods that will ensure that your copy is actually read. After all, it would be a terrible waste if you spent hours developing wonderful copy, packed full of carefully crafted, complex language patterns, only to discover that your readers didn't get past the headline. Believe me, that happens with most copy.

Finally, I show you how to write copy that captures attention, appeals to the requirements of your prospects and customers, keeps the attention of the reader and motivates that reader to complete a directed action.

The Golden Ratio

Let's start with the science. There is a number that is known as the 'Golden Ratio'. The number is a rather unexciting 0.618, which is almost exactly 8/13. (The number comes from the ratio 1:1.618, which is the same as 0.618:1.) It is also known as the 'Divine Proportion', and occasionally as 'Phi'. The common belief is that the name 'Phi' was given to this number as a result of its regular use by ancient Greek architect Phidias. He was one of the leading architects responsible for the design and construction of the Parthenon in Athens, Greece, which was built between 477 and 438 BC.

The Golden Ratio (the most common name for this number today) appears in several places in the Parthenon structure. The most obvious application of the Golden Ratio is to be found in its front aspect. It is exactly 0.618 times as high as it is wide. The footprint of the structure is a rectangle that utilises the Golden Ratio, and the central two pillars are exactly 0.618 times the width of the structure from each end (see illustration below).

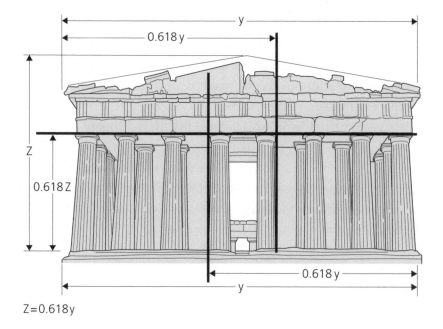

Z=0.618y

The Golden Ratio appears in architecture, art and music. The Great Pyramids at Giza, Egypt, are known to have been constructed intentionally using the Golden Ratio. In Mexico, ancient Aztec decorations very often used the Golden Ratio. Michelangelo used it to construct the life-size sculpture *David*, and Leonardo da Vinci actually documented applying it to his most famous paintings, calling it the 'Divine Proportion'.

Consider the application of the Golden Ratio to these paintings:

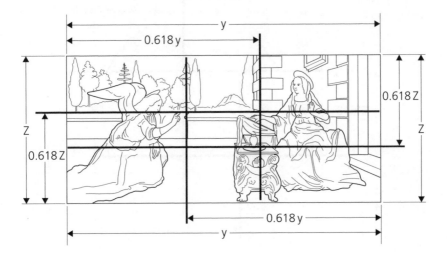

As can be clearly seen, Da Vinci chose to complete his painting using the Golden Ratio to mark out significant parts of the painting, and to align important objects. The result is that the painting is naturally attractive.

Now consider the Mona Lisa. Immediately notable is that the dimensions of the painting make use of the Golden Ratio. In order to maintain proper proportions, Da Vinci used the Golden Ratio to determine the head size, the neckline of the dress and the placement of the hands.

So where else can the Golden Ratio be found? Stradivarius documented how he used it to place the f-holes in his famous violins. An analysis of Mozart's sonatas found that they divide into two parts exactly at the Golden Ratio point in almost all cases, and his calculations of the ratio can be found scribbled on some of his orig-

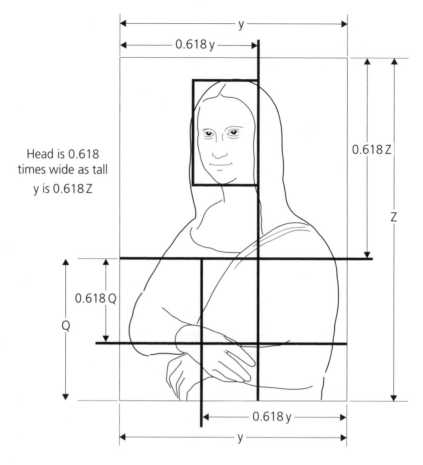

inal works. The Golden Ratio has also been used in the works of Beethoven, Bartok, Schubert, Bach, Debussy and Satie. While I accept that this may not have happened by design in every case, it is beyond coincidence that most musical masterpieces have applied the Golden Ratio.

There are individuals who claim that the Golden Ratio is a myth. My position is that whether it is scientifically proven or not, if it adds value to our marketing arsenal then we should consider its use. It is a fact that its application increases aesthetic pleasure, and that is a tool we can use.

I've personally tested the Golden Ratio within web pages, and within sales letters and marketing collateral. In my own tests, materials that utilised the Golden Ratio performed five or six times better than those materials that did not. It may not be conclusive scientific proof, but it's proven profitable for me – and could do for you, too.

To construct a letter using the Golden Ratio requires that you complete the following steps:

1. Measure and mark lines across the page that are 0.618 of the way up from the bottom, and 0.618 down from the top of the page. Also mark vertical lines in the same manner (see diagram below).

2. Measure and mark a line across the page that is 0.618 of the way up from the bottom of the page to the first horizontal line.

3. Measure and mark a line across the page that is 0.618 of the way down from the top of the page to the first horizontal line.

4. You should now have four horizontal lines. We will call them A, B, C and D – with A being the uppermost and D the lowest.

5. Line A should be where you place your headline.

6. Lines B and C should be where you place important benefits.

7. Line D should be where you place either a call to action, or your USP.

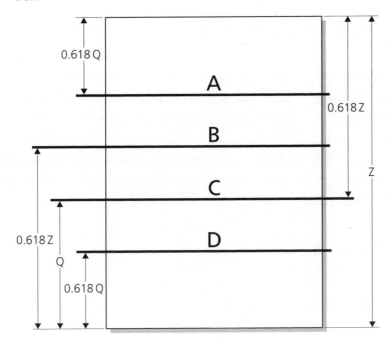

In my own tests I found no benefit in marking and using the Golden Ratio for vertical lines within sales or marketing letters. However, I did find a measurable improvement when using the vertical lines in web pages. I used the vertical lines to mark out images and significant copy, and my results showed that data retention was improved dramatically.

The Golden Ratio will be debated for many years to come. It is widely accepted as fact that its application increases aesthetic pleasure, but according to scientists, the fact that it also appears in nature means that it cannot be considered *the* most pleasing proportion – as they believe that nature often applies random components, and as such applying science could improve upon results found thus far.

Based upon my own testing, I choose to accept that the Golden Ratio improves the aesthetics of documents and does not devalue marketing materials in any way. As such, it is a powerful marketing weapon, and one that I will continue to use. You should test the Golden Ratio for yourself and if it improves readability and data retention, and increases your profits as a result, then I'm certain you'll feel much more confident in its use.

Essential points to cover in mailings

This list is one that I want you to learn. If you need to tattoo it on your body to guarantee you remember it, then do it. If you need to buy fridge magnets in order to place it somewhere that you'll never forget, then do so now. If you do not understand and accept this list, your direct mail will never reach its full potential. The list is packed full of pure profit. There are only four items on it, but each is literally worth millions.

1. **Headline** I cover this in detail below (see page 83), because it is *the* most important part of a letter.

2. **Benefits** Do not make your letter a data dump. If you have one exceptional benefit, just focus on that. Never detail more

than three benefits. I've seen letters that list eight or nine benefits, and it's a complete waste. Why? The human brain can only consciously focus on two, plus or minus one, items. Thus three benefits is your maximum, but one wonderful benefit is your goal.

3. **Risk reversal** This is a really powerful new Guerrilla Marketing weapon that I describe in detail in Chapter 10 (see page 141). It involves reducing the risk for prospects and customers by offering them benefits such as guarantees, warranties, pilot studies, samples, trial periods and deferred payment schemes. By shifting the element of risk to yourself, you reduce risk for the purchaser, which helps build their confidence in you.

4. **P.S.** I can't understand why more people do not use this weapon. Many studies have shown that a P.S. is the first part of any letter to be read in full (closely followed by the headline). What Guerrillas know is that the P.S. should be used to set the tone for the whole letter – as it will be read first. For example, 'P.S. Don't forget that you can use the 62 free Guerrilla Marketing weapons today!' That P.S. builds interest and intrigue, and offers a benefit that can be had today. More on this in Chapter 10 (see page 145).

Remember these items, and stick with them. There are only four of them to remember and each is essential to your direct mail success. If your marketing agency disagrees, get a new agency. It really is that important.

Using headlines

This is a very important strategy for you to employ in your written materials. I'm often challenged on this by individuals who believe that headlines have no place in formal letters. I argue that anything that improves the performance of the letter and increases profits should be included. Would you rather have a formal letter without a headline that delivers a 1 per cent response, or a formal letter with a headline that delivers a 14 per cent response? It's a no-brainer!

Guerrillas know that we should seek to differentiate our marketing materials, including letters, from those of our competitors. Your prospects probably get tens or hundreds of letters a month. Why should they read yours? A thumping great headline offering a wonderful benefit is a magnificent way of getting their attention.

I cannot emphasise enough the importance of a good headline. When I run my training courses I tell our delegates that when writing a letter, 90 per cent of the time should be spent creating and crafting a headline. This is not an exaggeration. If you have ten hours to construct a letter, spend nine hours on the headline.

The headline sets the tone for the whole letter. If the headline captures the attention of the reader, and they continue to read your copy, the headline has done its job. If you do not get the reader's attention, the rest of the letter is wasted. It doesn't matter how many presuppositions you've included, or how many embedded commands you've carefully constructed, you must get the reader's attention – and a good headline is the way.

When you scan through the pages of a newspaper, what captures your attention? It's just two things: images and headlines. Since we rarely use images in letters, headlines are the Guerrilla's chosen weapon for capturing attention.

Below are some very simple guidelines to creating a great headline. Follow these guidelines carefully and you'll find creative, profitable headlines come easy.

Questions work well

Before I continue, let me qualify this heading. *Open* questions (see also page 62) work well. An open question is one that cannot be answered 'yes' or 'no'. An open question requires interaction with the reader, and also requires that the reader goes through a derivation process to develop an answer. So rather than phrasing a question 'Can you make your mailing list profitable?' try, 'How can you make your mailing list profitable?'

The second form of question has two benefits; the first is that it is an open question, and so requires interaction through derivation. The second is that it brings value to the reader, as it suggests knowledge that they do not presently possess.

There is a risk in closed questions in that if a reader gives an unexpected answer, the conversation (and thus any interaction) is over. For example, 'Do your staff have problems with reaching decision makers?' may not be relevant if the reader is happy with his staff performance in reaching decision makers. The reader therefore says, in their head, 'No' and the conversation is over. If, however, you subtly turn the closed question into an open question, the response is more likely to be favourable. 'When do your staff have problems reaching decision makers?' is a much more effective question, as it is unlikely that they are always completely satisfied with the performance of their staff in reaching decision makers.

Arousing intrigue

People are naturally inquisitive. It's in our nature. Humans have an irresistible urge to learn, whether consciously or unconsciously. Using this knowledge in headlines is a wonderful weapon. Examples that have worked well in the past include:

'A little mistake that cost this farmer £20,000 a year . . .'

'How I started a new life with just £25.'

'How to do your Christmas shopping in five minutes.'

'The secret reason why people like you.'

Each of these headlines offers information that is not currently available to the reader, and as such is information that many readers would like to own. If you can create a headline that arouses similar interest, intrigue or fascination, then your headline is probably going to perform well.

Offering a solution

Everyone without exception has problems and challenges in their lives. If your product or service can make a reader's life easier by addressing and solving one of those problems, the reader will be ecstatic to read your copy if your headline details how you can provide a solution. I've already exposed the myth that people won't read long copy, so providing you have targeted your audience properly and offer a solution in a headline, you will very probably see a wonderful response to that headline. Examples include:

'Book your holiday today, with no deposit!'

'Reduce your manufacturing failure rates now!'

'How to win that tender'

Detailing an advantage

It is estimated that the average person is exposed to 30,000 marketing messages per day. Television, radio, email, buses, trains, taxis and billboards are just some of the marketing weapons used to arouse your purchasing gene. So how do you make sure your message is received and digested? There is one way and one way only – differentiate. If you take a look around at most marketing messages, they're actually pretty poorly constructed, and that's where your opportunity lies. If you can construct a headline that demands attention by detailing a benefit for the reader, and if they choose to deal with you, you have a winning headline.

People are bombarded all day by egocentric marketing messages. Prospects hardly care if you've been in business 25 years, if your clients include the Bank of England and Nike, or if your quality 'speaks for itself' – they care about what's in it for them. Why should they deal with you? What advantage is there for them? Give prospects a reason to deal with you. Explain what they will gain, how they will gain it and how the gain will benefit them – then tell them again and again. Just watch your profits soar. Examples include:

'Take advantage of our *no-questions-asked 100% money-back guarantee.*'

'If we don't succeed for you – you don't pay!'

'We deliver to you on time, or the delivery is free.'

Announcing some important news

This is actually another way of arousing curiosity. We all love news, and we all love to be the first to tell something. The risk in using this technique is that what you consider news may not be news for everyone else. Therefore you should only use news in a headline if it is genuinely news.

It is very important that you do not forget an important part of any information or benefits that you offer to prospects and customers – you must position it as a positive outcome. Guerrillas know that positioning a news headline that highlights a pain usually results in a negative response.

Make your headlines genuine news items and they will perform.

Borrowing from other headlines

Guerrillas know that to reinvent the wheel is usually a waste of resources. An excellent method for creating profitable headlines is to model the headlines of others. Take some time to study newspapers, industry publications and direct mailings. Soon you will notice certain types of headline that appear time and time again. Why? Because they work. Guerrillas take these headlines and create a file. Each time you find a headline structure that you've seen three or more times, put it in your file. Then, when you come to writing your own headlines, study the file and write a long list of headlines. Simply adjust the headlines to suit your needs by adding your own benefits and news items. This is not cheating – consider it Guerrilla Marketing efficiency.

Using written anchors and triggers

The next Guerrilla Marketing weapons that I want to present are written anchors and triggers. Although these weapons can be used in face-to-face meetings, it is easier to apply them (in the first instance at least) in written form.

I'm sure that at some point you've been in a situation where you were in a meeting with a client, had a wonderful state of rapport and everything was going swimmingly. Later in that same meeting, for some reason the atmosphere became strained or stress-laden. This could have been due to a miscommunication, a disagreement during the negotiation or some other reason, but you wished you'd had a means of rapidly reaccessing the wonderful state of rapport you had before. Anchors and triggers allow exactly that.

An anchor is any representation that triggers another representation. For example, the smell of a BarBQ might trigger a childhood memory of camping with your family. Another example might be a song or tune that triggers hilarious images of a wedding you once attended.

A trigger is a means of reaccessing a state that has already been anchored. In marketing collateral and sales letters, we often use words or phrases as triggers. So, we set the anchor by associating the chosen, and acquired, state with a word or phrase. Then, at a time when we wish to reaccess that state, we use that word or phrase again.

Earlier in this book I discussed the three main representational systems – visual, auditory and kinesthetic (see page 22). It is important for you to understand that when any part of an experience is reproduced, the other parts of that representation may also be reproduced. Therefore any part of a particular experience can be used as an anchor to access another portion of that experience.

In Guerrilla Marketing we use language to create anchors and then activate triggers. We do this because there are often single words that can elicit very strong positive and negative responses. When using the written word, Guerrillas also use italics and bold fonts to create anchors and activate triggers.

Creating an anchor is a four-stage process:

1. Develop a state that you wish to recreate later.

2. As the state is increasing in intensity, set the anchor.

3. Allow the state to subside.

4. Trigger the anchor.

Here is each stage explained in detail.

Develop a state that you wish to recreate later

Typically we only focus on states with positive outcomes. This is because we want our customers to feel great about everything that they associate with us. When a customer thinks about you and your organisation, they should have good memories about your high level of professionalism, your assistance in making the purchase easy and the great customer service you gave throughout – and afterwards. Therefore we only build states that make customers feel wonderful. Examples are excitement, comfort, intrigue and happiness. Use colourful language to build these states. In earlier chapters I presented you with methods for arousing intrigue and excitement – and these are great motivators for a buying decision. As such, they are excellent states to arouse. Open questions, clear benefits, promises and guarantees are all Guerrilla Marketing weapons that work well to create positive and useful states in your prospects and customers.

As the state is increasing in intensity, set the anchor

The more intense the experience that the reader is having when the anchor is set, the stronger the response will be when the trigger is activated. Therefore the lesson for novice Guerrillas is this: don't set the anchor too soon, and definitely don't set it too late. Always set the anchor just before the peak of the intensity, while still on the increase. For example:

As you read this letter you'll begin to get certain feelings of excitement as you realise that you can use 100 Guerrilla Marketing weapons that will bring you profit. Better still, you'll learn how to use the 62 FREE weapons. That's right! FREE marketing! *Think about it.* **You can use 62 FREE marketing weapons in your marketing today!**

In this example I've marked the anchor with italics. The anchor is set just before the most exciting statement in the example.

Allow the state to subside

Many copywriters will tell you that you should maintain 'the high' throughout a letter. They are wrong. If you honestly believe that you can maintain an unending high throughout a whole sales letter or marketing document, you are not a realist. Guerrillas are realists. Accept that the reader's mind will wander, and if you have written good copy, they will be considering your benefits and proposal. Using anchors is a means of controlling the tone of the copy. Do not be afraid to let the tone become less purchase inducing, as it is important that you provide the four necessary components of a sales letter – the headline, benefits, risk reversal and P.S. (see page 82).

Trigger the anchor

In the example of an anchor provided above, the anchor was 'Think about it'. As simple as it may seem, to activate the trigger all you need to do is use exactly the same term, at a time and place in the letter where you want to reaccess the state you created before. It sounds straightforward – and it is. Contrary to common belief, anchors do not need to be repeated many times to allow them to 'sink in'. The unconscious mind is incredibly astute and can form associations quicker than you would think possible. That said, repeating the anchoring process can reinforce an anchor – but in a letter it is overkill, and reduces the covert nature of the anchoring process. Keep it subtle. We don't want readers to feel that we are tricking them. Guerrilla Marketing has embraced this and many other advanced methods to increase communication effectiveness. We have no interest in stealth marketing.

The methods described in this chapter are not theories – they genuinely work in the real world. I know because I use them daily and so do my clients. Try them, but do so slowly. If you try to apply everything you've just discovered in one letter today, the result will probably be a mess. These weapons and methods take time to become second nature to you. Practise and test them. Then test some more.

I will leave you with one final thought regarding writing for the unconscious mind. When you read any material, you hear a voice in your head. Usually it is your own voice, and it's perfectly natural. The same is true of every prospect and customer that reads your copy. They all hear your copy in their heads. So, write your copy with that in mind. Make it personal and make it conversational. People don't like to be talked at. They like to think that your copy has been written for them, and that you're comfortable speaking to them in an informal tone. Write as you would speak to a friend – and never forget to write for profit.

CHAPTER 7

Congruence and Your Marketing Identity

ONE AFTERNOON I had a problem with my Internet connection. A brief investigation showed that it was an issue with my Internet service provider (ISP). I telephoned the company and was greeted by an automated message telling me, 'Your call is important to us and will be answered as soon as a representative is available. Please hold.'

Content that my call was important, I decided to hold. Some 20 minutes later, having heard the same message 20 times at one-minute intervals, I began to question the integrity of the woman on the answer message. If my call was important, why had I been ignored for 20 minutes?

Soon, my concerns were validated as I was greeted by another automated message, 'Sorry, but all of our representatives are busy. Please call again later.' A singular click confirmed that my call had been terminated. Surely not? My call was important to them – the lady said so!

Frustrated, I tried again. Once again for 20 minutes I was on hold, then my call was dropped. A terrible thought struck me – my call wasn't important to the company at all! They'd simply told me that to placate me.

Now frustrated and angry, I called the complaints department.

Once again I was greeted by an automated response explaining how important my call was, and how I would be answered as soon as a representative was available. Another 20 minutes later, still unanswered and following repeats of the message at one-minute intervals, I was addressed by an automated message, 'I'm sorry. Nobody is available to take your call. Please leave a message after the tone.'

At last I felt that someone would hear my complaint. I waited for the tone, then heard a message that made me even angrier than before: 'Message box full. Goodbye.' The now familiar click confirmed that once again my call had been dropped.

I reviewed the day's events in my head. The company had failed to provide the service for which I was paying. They then failed to provide the technical support for which I was paying. They then were unable to take my call. Finally, when I had got through to the complaints department, they already had so many complaints that the voicemail message box was full! Their message had said that my call was important to them and I felt hoodwinked, as my call was clearly not important to them at all.

Needless to say, I cancelled my account the same day. There are numerous ISPs who are willing to provide a high level of service, remaining attentive throughout any problems that may arise. I need a company that I can trust.

Marketing is harder now than ever before. You have more competitors than at any other time in the past, and customers are more demanding too. More importantly, prospects and customers are more street-wise than at any other time in history. The Internet allows prospects to research their preferred product or service on a global scale, and as a result your target market is very well educated about your offerings. The bad news is that because so many scam artists have already marketed to your prospects and customers, your honesty and reliability are in question at all times, even to existing customers. Your marketing identity, and congruence with that identity (that is, maintaining a consistent and predictable identity in everything you do), is among your most powerful marketing weapons – if they are used well.

Your marketing identity

Let's be clear. Identity is not the same as image. An image is created and projected. Guerrillas often call an image an 'elective state', as it is a position that has been chosen to be projected, regardless of its relevance or accuracy. An identity, on the other hand, is the reality of your market positioning and levels of service, projected through congruence. It is the manner in which you conduct business, and is most accurately determined by asking the opinion of your existing customers.

The market is full of organisations which project a marketing image that suits their own needs. The problem is that very many of the same companies fail to maintain congruency through their marketing and customer management. For example, there are organisations that project a caring and attentive image, and then send irrelevant automated responses to your letters, charge you for the attention they promised and utilise automated telephone systems that make business easier for them and more difficult for you. That is not congruent with the corporate image, which in turn is definitely not their identity.

Working for the client

Guerrillas know that organisations should be run for the convenience of their clients. There are eight ways in which Guerrillas ensure that marketing campaigns are congruent with an honest corporate identity, while respecting market intellect and maintaining profitability.

1. Only contact clients when you have something new to say

Calling clients to 'touch base' or 'see what's happening' does not make them feel special, and is not a good reason to contact them. Contact clients when you see articles or white papers that may be relevant to them, or when you are about to release a newsletter. (Maybe even send VIP clients a pre-release issue?) If your organisation has just completed a deal with a similar company, call the client to tell them about it.

Every contact you ever have with any client should bring value to the call, letter or email. The result is that the client looks forward to your calls and correspondence. If you find that a client is seldom available to take your call, and rarely returns calls when requested to do so, you need to look at the value of the conversations you offer the contact. Respect your clients' time and only interrupt their busy day when you genuinely have something relevant to tell them.

2. Make it easy for your clients to do business with you

Clients do not have time to waste trying to find a 'checkout' link on your website, and they expect you to take all major credit cards (regardless of the transaction costs that must be absorbed). Clients are the reason you have a business. The more clients you have, and the more regularly they order, the bigger your business will grow. Your business should not be run for your own convenience. If you don't want to work weekends, that's fine, but make sure you employ someone who does – some clients will want to order at weekends. Also bear in mind that the technology is available to permit you to automate your business, and take orders 24 hours a day, seven days a week.

Are your employees familiar with all your products and services, to the degree that they can answer all customers' queries? If they are not, you can bet that your competitors' employees are, and that's where your prospects will go. Many websites and brochures are poorly designed as they have been created with aesthetics rather than function in mind. If your website designer tells you that a spinning 'welcome' animation will make your website more effective, get a new designer. Yes, your website should be attractive to look at, but not at the cost of functionality. When Guerrillas send emails to clients announcing offers and sales, they insert the link to the actual page, not just the homepage. (That may seem an obvious thing to do, but the majority of businesses do not do it!) The easier it is for clients to do business with you, the more clients will do business with you.

3. Stress your USP in *everything* you do

Most successful businesses are built around a single USP. You don't need four or five USPs, but if you have them then select the most powerful one and tell the whole world. Differentiation is the key to modern marketing. Your USP is the reason why your offering cannot be placed in a spreadsheet that compares prices alone. One reason why many businesses fail is that they allow apples to be compared to apples – they simply position their own apples as the best-value or best-quality apples. Where others are selling apples, Guerrillas aim to sell a delicious, magical fruit that tastes like an apple and possesses all the character traits of an apple, yet has never been seen before, has less waste and is always perfectly ripe. Don't sell apples.

4. Employ complete and total honesty

Guerrillas know the public has access to information that was never available before. Honesty is a necessary Guerrilla trait, as a client who discovers a damaging secret will tell five or six times more people than a client who discovers a pleasant secret. If you have a sale, explain the reason for it. For example, if a customer postpones an order and you are left with some time-sensitive stock, tell your prospects exactly that and offer it to them at a reduced price. Your prospects will be amazed at your honesty, and even if they don't order in this instance, they are more likely to order in the future. (The ideal strategy is to package the reduced stock with existing stock at your regular prices, the sales point being something like, for example, 'Get 200 widgets at 30 per cent off when you order 50 thingies.') Every one of my clients who has used this method has profited.

Never be afraid to confront your organisation's weaknesses.

Guerrillas know that inoculation can turn a weakness into a benefit. Remember inoculations (see page 63)? I told you they had many powerful uses, and this is just one more to add to your arsenal. Tell prospects that you are aware of your weaknesses and that you are addressing them. How many of your competitors say, 'Our delivery times are really poor' to their prospects and customers? I'm willing to bet none of them do. However, Guerrillas are unafraid of the truth, so a Guerrilla might say to a prospect, 'Our competitors may have told you that our delivery times are poor, and at the moment that is true. However, we offer a 'track-and-trace' facility on our website, so you can access that free of charge and you will always know where your delivery is, and you can plan around that. Also, our delivery times are continually improving.' With that inoculation in place, the prospect is very unlikely to mention poor delivery times. Guerrillas know that honesty is a wonderful weapon.

5. Understand and address customers' needs

One of the biggest misconceptions in modern sales and marketing is that we should supply customers with whatever they want or believe they need. This is simply not true. Honesty is a Guerrilla trait, so if a customer suggests to you that they need a particular product or service and you know this to be untrue, even if you sell that product or service, you absolutely must make the customer aware of the information that makes you believe otherwise. This may well talk you out of a sale, but Guerrillas know that building relationships with customers through trust is more important than closing deals.

Consider this scenario. A customer contacts you to ask about buying some widgets. His staff have been to a trade show and decided that they absolutely require some widgets. As an industry expert, you know that you can sell this customer some widgets, but you also know that they are not the best fit for the application he has in mind. Now, a true Guerrilla would tell the customer about the inappropriate purchase, presenting supporting data to validate the claim. However, for this scenario let's assume that you don't. Instead, you sell the client some widgets, and make a good margin.

Six months later, you receive a telephone call from the customer. One of your competitors has just had a meeting with him, and shown him data that shows the widgets are a poor fit for his application. To corroborate the data, the customer had his staff research the other options available and decided that your competitor is correct – the widgets that you sold to him are not a good fit for the application. Suddenly this customer now doubts your expertise and your commitment to his organisation, and questions your agenda; worst of all, he now doubts your honesty.

Now let's assume you'd applied proper Guerrilla practice, and told the customer about the lack of best fit. This would have helped build rapport with the customer, even though you may not have won the sale. Additionally, it would have helped validate your perceived expertise, confirmed your commitment to the customer and shown that you are trustworthy, even in the face of a lost sale.

Your customers' needs must always, without exception, be addressed. When you calculate the net worth of a customer to your organisation over a period of five years, and then ten years, you will see that it is worth investing in that customer. If you fail to address customers' needs, they will go and find someone else who will. If customers tell you that they need 24-hour customer service, give it to them. If they tell you that they need better delivery times, provide them. Claiming to be a customer-focused organisation and then failing to identify and meet customer needs is incongruent and will cost you thousands or possibly millions.

6. Recognise who your customers are

I've said this in previous Guerrilla Marketing books and I'll say it again – advertising does not work. This may seem illogical, unlikely or just plain incredible to you, so let me explain. Advertising on its own does not work and is not a good investment. That said, if you include advertising as a weapon within a larger marketing campaign that includes multiple weapons (telemarketing, direct mail, trade shows, postcards, and so on), advertising could be a very powerful weapon indeed.

As a rule, companies who are trying to sell you advertising do not have any financial interest in your success. They run your advert and take your money, regardless of performance. That's fair enough – it's their business. However, advertising is typically a numbers game and Guerrilla Marketing is not. Guerrillas use advertising, but only as part of a combination of marketing weapons, and only as an intensely focused weapon.

Within your marketing arsenal, advertising should be considered the sniper's rifle. During conflict, snipers do not spray bullets at groups hoping to hit a high-value target. Snipers wait, sometimes for weeks, to fire just one shot at a carefully selected target. They often study their target for a lengthy period of time before deciding how and when to engage that target, and when the time is right they fire with deadly precision. However, a sniper cannot win a war alone. Support from other units, and weapons, is required.

Not only should you know who your customers are, but also that they now expect you to know their habits. Your advertising needs to be focused with laser precision. For example, if your primary prospects are London commuters, your advertisement headline should read, 'If you commute to London daily, etc.' This displays a thorough understanding of your target audience, and is congruent with a professional marketing company that understands its customers. Guerrillas avoid headlines and advertisements that are ambiguous or non-specific.

7. Be consistent and predictable in your marketing

There have been many studies conducted across countless industries to determine the priorities and buying criteria of purchasers. Almost without exception, the top reason that purchasers give for choosing a particular vendor is 'trust'. The modern customer seeks high value and low risk. In most studies, 'price' only ranks fourth or fifth in the list of priorities, therefore fuelling the argument that sales and marketing professionals are more obsessed with price than most customers are.

There are a myriad of organisations that come to mind that have built up a well-respected and trusted brand and then attempted to launch another similar range using the same branding, and watched it fail miserably. A notable case is one particular large, high-profile training shoe manufacturer. Their brand was proven, profitable and trusted. On the back of this success, they decided to launch a range of athletic clothing. It failed sorrowfully, and at a huge cost to the company. The range was cancelled and the post-mortem began. After six months of research, it was shown that the range had been rejected because the market had always seen and trusted the company as manufacturers of great training shoes. The corporate identity was that of a dependable manufacturer, with a celebrated track record in high-quality training shoes, not athletic equipment or clothing. The company had tried to portray a brand image that extended to expertise in athletic clothing, and it was just that – an image. It wasn't real, and it wasn't how the public saw the brand.

At the neurological level, the brain is most comfortable with what it already knows, and it learns quickest from anything new. Guerrillas know this and use it to its best advantage. If you can introduce new information and images to trigger familiar associations in the unconscious mind of your prospects and customers, then you can penetrate their minds more quickly than any traditional marketing methods could ever hope to.

Maintain consistency in your marketing. Keep a familiar feel in everything you do throughout every marketing campaign, as this will comfort your customers. A sudden change in direction will worry and confuse customers, and suddenly your organisation will be seen as higher risk, as the familiar feeling has gone. It is a sad fact that most successful marketing campaigns are cancelled too early. I've been in many marketing meetings where a committee has decided that a campaign needs to be changed, just because 'it is getting old'. If the campaign is still profitable, and the customers are still buying, leave it alone! The Marlboro cowboy has been smoking the same brand, profitably, for 50 years. Why? Because the market likes it that way, and the marketing team at Marlboro are smart enough to leave a profitable campaign alone.

8. Use precision persuasion

Traditional marketing makes extensive use of absolute terms such as biggest, quickest and longest. Guerrillas know that using such terms is dangerous, and instead use intentionally precise language to explain benefits and USPs in a manner that creates kinesthetic sensations and images in the minds of prospects and customers. The only time to use absolute terms is when you can present undeniable proof to support a claim. If there is any doubt that your widget is the quickest or smallest, don't make the claim, because it only takes one competitor to prove otherwise and your identity as an honest professional is suddenly being questioned. As a Guerrilla, your identity should always be that of a caring and considerate professional, who could provide accurate information upon request. Getting caught using inaccurate absolute terms is not congruent with this identity. Before you can even begin to persuade your prospects and customers, you must build rapport, so be precise in everything that you offer to your target market.

As discussed and demonstrated in earlier chapters, language patterns and their delivery are key in precision persuasion. Then again, complex embedded command structures and ambiguities are of absolutely no use at all unless you have the attention of the audience, and this is exactly where many marketing campaigns fall flat on their faces. Remember, you can forget advertising and any other Guerrilla Marketing weapon, strategy or technique, *unless your product or service is interesting*. If you can't make your offering interesting, you will not be able to market it effectively. No ifs or buts. You unconditionally must offer a product or service that demands the attention of your audience. When you have the attention that your offering requires and deserves, you can go about your precision persuasion. The more attentive your audience, the more precise you can be. In turn, this will also reduce the length of the decision-making process, as an interested mind can be easily directed and persuaded.

Whether you already have a corporate identity that you are considering, or are about to create an identity for your organisation, bear in mind that an identity should last a lifetime. Your identity may evolve over a period of many years, but you need to assume that the identity you create now will stay with you for ten years at least. Once you are happy with your identity, make certain that all your marketing activity and collateral supports it. I cannot emphasise enough the importance of congruence. If you present an identity to the market and then all your marketing activity reinforces the identity, the market will freely accept that identity. Conversely, if you do not reinforce the identity and your marketing campaigns present a new or different image, your identity will be questioned, and finally rejected.

If you can't present a cohesive marketing identity in everything that you do, why should the market accept your positioning? The fact is they won't. If the market recognises any incongruence in your marketing it will establish your position for you, and that will be very expensive for your organisation. It's your bus; do you want to be a passenger?

Make Marketing Success a Habit

E ACH OF THE FOLLOWING words is commonly used in relation to modern Guerrilla Marketing, and is associated with characteristics that are of key importance to it:

Patience
Commitment
Consistency
Predictability
Simple
Aggressive
Action
Language
Learning
Model
Change
Focus
Gifts
Profit

I have studied many successful and profitable Guerrilla Marketing campaigns, and have modelled the top performers in the marketing world. Without exception, the leading marketing managers, directors and gurus all understand and make use of the above in their work and other parts of their lives – and you should too.

To gain the full benefit of these items, you must first completely understand how and why each item is important, and then how to successfully apply all of them in your life.

Patience

This is without doubt the singularly most important trait that any marketer must possess. Without patience you cannot be a true Guerrilla, but more worryingly, you will rarely achieve success in your marketing. Lack of patience has ruined more potentially brilliant marketing campaigns than any other single factor.

I have already discussed the repetition strategy that has long been the backbone of Guerrilla Marketing (see page 67). The strategy was built upon a research study which showed that a prospect's mind needs to be penetrated as many as nine times to move that prospect from total apathy to the purchasing decision. The study also found that for every three presentations of your marketing message, the prospect would only see it once – so you actually need to present your message 27 times.

Consider the patience required to present a marketing message 27 times. It might be weeks, months or possibly even years. Do you have the patience to wait that long for the order? If you don't yet, you need to develop your precision persuasion skills (see page 101). These skills will often shorten the sales cycle, and allow you to gain consent for further marketing to your prospects and customers. However, even the precision persuasion skill set is limited by one simple fact, and that is that people are people, not robots. If I could accurately predict how each and every prospect and customer was going to react, this book would be in the occult section in most major bookshops. What we can do, however, is increase the accuracy of our testing by using psychology and the precision persuasion skill set.

Regardless of your strategies, methods and selection of weapons, and the delivery of your marketing thrust, you absolutely must have patience in your marketing. This is a trait found in all the top performers in sales and marketing throughout the world. The reason for this is clear: by seeking to persuade, you are actually asking prospects to examine their own beliefs, consider your information and trust you enough to make a purchasing decision – which may mean changing an existing belief. Although changing a belief takes a fraction of a second, developing the trust to use your information to do so takes time. Be patient and reap the rewards.

Commitment

This is, unfortunately, the least abundant trait in professional marketers, outside of Guerrilla Marketing. I have seen hundreds of product and campaign launches where sales and marketing staff are so motivated and enthusiastic that if you could bottle it, you'd make millions. The problem is that six months down the line the mood has invariably changed. For whatever reason, the forecasted figures have not been met (usually due to poor forecasting). As a result, someone somewhere has had the 'great' idea of relaunching or rebranding the offering. Therefore the first problem here is lack of patience.

Consider the 'Marlboro Cowboy' and 'Flavor Country' campaigns. It took over a year to show any measurable effect, yet has remained profitable for 53 years.

In most industries, regardless of what your advertising agency tells you (after all, their job is to sell advertising) six months is not enough time to cause a shift in habit or brand for most people. There are exceptions, but these cost many millions. Since the majority of marketing campaigns do not have that type of budget available, we need to focus on strategies that utilise more typical budgets.

The least expensive way of ensuring that your marketing campaign is a profitable success is a five-stage process:

1. Research your market thoroughly and completely.

2. Develop a Guerrilla Marketing plan based on your research.

3. Test your plan, and make adjustments where needed.

4. Launch your attack with commitment.

5. Commit to the attack and maintain a ruthless barrage of your marketing message and USP.

The Guerrilla Marketing Plan (stage 2 above) is only 7 sentences!

The first tells the purpose of your marketing.
The second tells how to achieve the purpose, stressing benefits.
The third tells what your target audience or audiences are.
The fourth details which weapons you'll use.
The fifth tells your niche in the market place. You need a niche.
The sixth describes your identity – not your image, but identity.
The seventh tells your marketing budget as a % of gross sales.

It really is that simple! If your marketing plan is any more complicated than that, then you're diluting the message.

Many organisations complete the first four stages adequately. The reason why many organisations fail is because they are unable or unwilling to action the fifth stage.

There are two very frustrating things that I see in almost every organisation when I provide my first consultancy.

Scenario one

This is a scenario that I'm sure you are familiar with.

The organisation develops a new product. Managers, directors and staff representatives spend hours in meetings devising strategies and marketing messages that their research indicates will help the product launch. Thousands of pounds are spent on new marketing materials, posters, adverts, flyers and brochures. The company is buzzing with enthusiasm and excitement.

Six months later, the product is withdrawn because sales are not as expected. Some sales staff are fired, others resign before they are pushed.

Managers, directors and staff representatives start over and spend hours in meetings devising strategies and marketing messages that their research indicates will help the new product launch. Again, thousands of pounds are spent on new marketing materials, posters, adverts, flyers and brochures.

And so the cycle continues.

It is startling how many companies operate in this manner. This type of cycle is partially responsible for the fact that the average sales manager in the UK moves from one company to another every 14 months.

Scenario two

This scenario may also be familiar to you.

The organisation has a profitable product, which maintains good market share. The product has been in the market for five years, and has always shown a profit. However, someone within the marketing department believes that the product has grown 'stale' and needs 'freshening up'. As a result, the product is relaunched – and fails. The marketing department puts this down to 'a shift in market trends'.

Staying with a marketing campaign

There are two important lessons to be gained here. In the first scenario, the organisation would have saved time and money if it had simply committed to the plan that it had taken all the time, effort and resources to develop. In most industries, six months is not long enough to allow a marketing campaign to fully flourish. Commit to the plan. Stick with it. Be relentless, and understand this: even an average marketing plan executed with commitment will outperform a brilliant marketing plan developed without commitment – *every* time.

In the second scenario, someone should have asked the marketing department, 'If you believe the product has gone stale, why is it still profitable?' Profitable marketing campaigns should be left alone. The Marlboro cowboy has been smoking profitably for 53 years. Is that campaign stale? The Jolly Green Giant has been 'Ho Ho Ho'ing' profitably for 30 years. Is that campaign stale? Let me be very clear on this: a campaign is only stale when it ceases to be profitable.

Now let me let you in on another secret. Marketing departments get bored with campaigns before the market does. This is due partly to poor market research and measurement of marketing weapons, and partly to the department's perceived need to account for itself. For example, if a product you launched tomorrow was profitable and continued to be profitable three years from now, even though you haven't changed the marketing campaign, don't you think your bosses would ask what exactly you do all day? That is the reason why many profitable campaigns are shelved early – poor management and weak marketing departments.

Great marketers know that commitment to a campaign is the key to success. If it's not profitable yet, but you know you've completed everything properly, continue the marketing attack. Once it is profitable, leave it alone.

Create with longevity in mind, and commit to profitable excellence.

Consistency

As already discussed (see page 99), to make a purchasing decision a prospect needs to feel that they can trust you and feel safe in knowing that what you say is accurate, and intended with their best interests in mind.

The problem comes when you, or your organisation, become incongruent. When your marketing messages and your behaviours, positioning or identity do not match, prospects have a real problem in deciding which is the 'true' you. To reduce this risk you must maintain consistency in everything you do. Everyone should answer the phone the same way. Everyone should learn the same 'elevator pitch' (a 20-second description of the benefits your organisation offers). Everyone should introduce the same USP and know the history of the company and its management structure. Signatures at the bottoms of emails should be the same for all staff, using identical layout and formats for telephone numbers. Procedures should be in place to ensure that all client-facing documentation is strictly regulated, to maintain consistency in appearance and quality.

This may seem like overkill – until you try it. You will see a difference in the market's perception of your organisation. At the unconscious level, the market will see you as a more secure, lower risk organisation. At the conscious level you will be perceived as having increased your professionalism. We don't fully understand why, but our research has shown that the vast majority of people associate regimentation with professionalism.

Predictability

This is actually a result of the three previous terms, and should not be confused with guesswork. If you are patient with your marketing and committed to your marketing plan, you only need to focus on consistency to ensure predictability. If your marketing is patient, committed and consistent, you will see your marketing become more predictable, the longer the campaign continues.

I need to refer to patience again here. Your marketing will become more predictable, but will never be completely predictable. That said, initially you may not see very much predictability at all. You must be patient. As your campaign runs its course, if you continue to measure and test your selection of weapons and headlines, you will soon find that you are able to accurately predict certain facets of your marketing campaign. This is the Holy Grail of professional marketers.

Simple

Whenever I am engaged in consultancy and present a Guerrilla Marketing plan, I almost always hear the client say, 'That's so simple.' Sometimes my clients even say, 'That seems just too simple.'

A key underpinning of Guerrilla Marketing has always been the desire to demystify marketing. If you briefly glance over the plethora of marketing books in any bookshop, you will find that the bulk of the offerings promise to share 'secrets'. As I've already said in this book, there are no secrets. I've personally been involved with marketing campaigns created for some of the world's largest companies, and have been involved in some incredibly successful campaigns – and I didn't need any secrets.

Marketing should be simple. If you do a small number of things well, and then measure your results, your campaign will be profitable. It sounds too simple – and it's supposed to be. Don't believe the secrecy merchants.

Aggressive

This is where it gets difficult. The non-adversarial, positive-outcome-based methods that I've already presented in this book do not lend themselves freely to aggression, yet aggression is a personality trait to be found in all successful Guerrilla Marketers. So how does it work? You need a very subtle balance between your aggression and your soft steps, and that is the skill in modern Guerrilla Marketing.

Aggression is a good thing, if channelled well. Where should you direct your aggression? There are a number of places where aggression is not just desired, but necessary to maximise your profits. For example, you need to be aggressive about every single penny you spend. When the magazine agrees to discount an advertising slot for you to only £700, tell them your budget is only £600, but that if the advert performs well you will advertise regularly. I can tell you right now, if they really want your business, they can afford to further discount. It might mean only a saving of £100 in this example, but if you save that amount every month that's £1,200 a year, and over a five-year period you will save £6,000.

You also need to be aggressive about follow-up, defining procedures, business discipline, maintaining consistency and seeking profit. These are just some of the places where you need to be aggressive, and if you look hard into your marketing activity I'm certain you'll find many more places where additional aggression will translate into profit. Start your search now.

Taking action

Whenever I conduct a training seminar, it is frustrating for me to know that very few of the delegates in the room will actually apply any of the strategies and methods I'm offering. It amazes me that intelligent business professionals will pay to see what Guerrilla Marketing is all about, and then decide not to use the newly gained knowledge that they paid for. I want this to be very clear: Guerrilla Marketing is not a spectator sport.

It doesn't matter what skills you have, what strategies you devise or how many language patterns you learn, if you do not take action your marketing will not be profitable. If you read the work of any of the top business gurus, they all say the same thing. Tony Robbins, Jay Abraham, Dr Bandler, Steven Covey, Brian Tracey and many others all insist that 'action' is the missing component in most business professionals' lives.

Admit it – how many times have you bought a personal-development or business book, read it and thought that it was a brilliant idea, then done nothing about it? The chances are that you've done it more than once. I freely admit that I used to do this, and then I decided I wasn't successful enough for my own liking. I raised the bar, and demanded better performance of myself. I decided that trying some of the methods I'd developed was the way forward. The result? Less stress, a better lifestyle and profit, profit, profit!

Now it's your turn. Get a piece of paper right now. Go on. Go and get a piece of paper. I'll still be here when you get back. Write down ten things you are going to try in the next ten days. Go back through the chapters you've already read, pick out your ten favourite ideas or strategies, and list them on the piece of paper. Once you've drawn up your list (this is the important bit), write next to each item the day on which you are going to apply that idea or skill. Don't fudge. 'Next week' is not specific enough. 'Monday morning' is better. When you've completed your list and assigned times for application, read on.

Using language

As long as you remember that every word in language creates an image in your prospect's mind, and that image will not be the same as your image, language is a wonderful marketing weapon.

What you must not do is believe that language alone can bring you sales. Like any other Guerrilla Marketing weapon, language does not typically perform well as a lone weapon, but when combined it will be a winner.

When I conduct my follow-up sessions with clients who have attended my 'Guerrilla Marketing Practitioner' course, I invariably find that the weapon most overused is language. During the training, it is very apparent how powerful persuasive language patterns can be. The problem comes when the newly qualified practitioners fail to recognise, or remember, that applying language patterns is not about being smarter than your prospects and customers, but about improving communications expertise.

The language patterns introduced in this book are not designed to enable you to win sales by stealth. I am not interested in tricking clients. Every single language pattern that I've highlighted for you is intended to improve the clarity of your marketing message. It is when, and only when, you understand and accept this, that you should begin to experiment with language as a marketing weapon.

Learning

Here we return to the age-old problem of the 'I know' syndrome. The two most dangerous words in sales and marketing today are 'I know'. Parts of the Guerrilla Marketing arsenal have been utilised in marketing elsewhere, as Guerrilla Marketing accepts that certain elements in traditional marketing strategies are sound in principle. Whenever I provide consultancy, I can be certain that at some point the client is going to say, 'I know.' In essence, this is not a problem. However, 'I know' actually means, 'I know that already so I'm not going to apply it, because it isn't brand new to me.' That is a problem. Just because you are aware of a marketing strategy does not mean that you understand it or how to best apply it. Some knowledge is often more dangerous than none.

Humans are instinctively driven to seek out new information – to learn. When I collect my son from school I don't ask, 'What did you do today?' Instead, I ask, 'What did you learn today?' This may only be a subtle linguistic change, but it allows him to recognise that he did actually learn something, as he must go through a personal derivation of his activities to highlight an item that he believed he learned.

So my question to you now is, 'What have you learned today?'

Model

There is a misconception that to model someone or something is to mimic it. I have often had to explain to my students that to blindly mimic a person is not modelling.

The word 'model' comes from the Latin *modulus*, which essentially means a small version of the original mode. In Guerrilla Marketing, the value of any type of modelling is its usefulness. Theories are great, but useful methods are more profitable.

To copy someone's activities, habits or traits is not modelling, as you do not learn how and why that person behaves in that way. To truly model behaviour, you must identify and provide a description of what is required to actually achieve a similar result. Only when you can do so will you be able to transfer that behaviour to others. That is our goal in Guerrilla Marketing.

To accurately model someone, you must be skilled in asking intelligent questions, as the quality of your questions will determine the quality of the answers you get. To complete the modelling process, you must also be aware of non-verbal behaviours.

For example, Michael Jordan would often stick out his tongue during times of stress or concentration whilst playing in the NBA, but if you simply stuck out your tongue when playing basketball, would that improve your performance? Unlikely. However, if we could find out what Michael Jordan was thinking, what he was visualising and what his internal dialogue was saying to him, then suddenly his tongue sticking out would have some value for us.

Modelling exceptional performance is a great tool that we have embraced in modern Guerrilla Marketing. Learn how to model people properly, and practise the skill. Once you have the skills necessary to model others, suddenly that model becomes transferable to anyone who wishes – even you.

Using change

It is an absolutely undeniable fact that some people are afraid of change. Others, on the other hand, like to regularly change things for no business reason other than personal opinion. Guerrillas seek a balance.

Change is at the basis of both evolution and destruction. As a result, change can be either a resource or a problem, and Guerrillas seek the former. Decisions based around change should be simple in marketing. If something is not profitable, you must consider changing it. (Note that I haven't said you must change it, but that you must consider change.) The flip side of that argument is that if something is profitable you should not change it, regardless of peer pressure.

Guerrilla Marketing campaigns often find success through their ability to remain flexible, due to good design in the first instance. Change is an excellent means of maintaining not just flexibility but velocity too. For example, if a marketing weapon is clearly not performing, and analysis has shown that the weapon (rather than the audience) is the problem, a rapid change of weapon is an excellent strategy.

The top-performing marketing professionals have all shown that they are unafraid of change, yet will make rapid changes following study and measurement. What we can also learn from the same marketing professionals is that change for the sake of 'newness' is rarely a good business decision. So, never dismiss change without analysis, but always make your decision with profit as the benchmark.

Maintaining focus

Creating a marketing plan can be simple. Launching a Guerrilla Marketing attack is slightly more difficult. Maintaining the attack is much more difficult. But the most difficult of all Guerrilla Marketing skills is maintaining focus.

As the marketing plan succeeds and profits amass, it is easy to get drawn away from the initial plan in search of further profits. The ability to continue with the same focus as was present at the launch of the campaign is the sign of a true Guerrilla. It is not easy. To stray from the proven path is so much easier than chasing new fields of profit. Publishing companies will offer you 'great advertising deals' in industry publications, unplanned trade show opportunities will arise and joint ventures outside of your plans will beg for funding. You must resist.

You must maintain your focus with reference to all of your resources, including funding, time, effort, imagination and human resources. If you allow your focus to broaden, two things happen:

1. **Your resources become thinly spread** The worst possible scenario is that you pay so much attention to the new project that the existing projects, weapons and clients are treated with indif-

ference. Incidentally, this is also what usually happens in this situation.

2. **Your existing marketing plan becomes strained** After all, it wasn't designed with the new opportunity in mind. In fact, in most cases the opportunity will be a bad fit for the existing plan.

As the power of the Internet increases, focus becomes more important than ever before. Prospects have never been so well informed, or so choosy. So, you need to become a big fish in your own little pond, not be a small fish in a big ocean. Guerrillas seek to dominate their own niche market, as there is more profit in that model than in picking up scraps from the larger market.

To summarise: find a niche and develop a strong focus. Once you have that focus, maintain it. Focus leads to profit.

Presenting Gifts

As I've already explained, it's in the psychological make-up of humans that when we are given a gift, we carry an unconscious feeling of debt towards the gift giver. Gifts are an element of Guerrilla Marketing that has always been considered a powerful weapon within the arsenal. In Guerrilla Marketing we treat each client relationship like a relationship with a partner, with whom we seek intimacy. That's right, Guerrilla Marketing is like sex.

Let me introduce four types of male, each seeking intimacy with the female form. Each type can be directly compared to a type of marketer. If you are male, you need to decide which of these models describes your marketing style. If you're female then you may have been approached by any or all of these models, so you'll easily understand and relate to this metaphor.

The first type is the **schoolboy**. He is anxious to have sex, but he doesn't care who with or how he gets it. He has little experience, and his brash methods clearly display this. His lack of subtlety and lack of focus on prime candidates mean that his success rates are low. He does occasionally win a sexual victory, but because he doesn't truly understand his partner, the level of satisfaction for her is low.

The second type is the **college graduate**. He's more experienced than the schoolboy. He's a sexual athlete who has picked up some 'tricks' that win him victories. He understands that some patience is required, but more often than not he prefers the quick win rather than the satisfying relationship. He begrudges spending on gifts because he knows that easy victories are available elsewhere. When the sexual victory is won, he loses interest in his conquest and moves on.

The third type is the **happily married man**. He is content to have regular sex with his chosen partner. Twice a week, with the lights off – that's the way he likes it. He's always done it that way and he feels a security in the safety of repetition. He doesn't seek sex elsewhere, and he's happy to plod on with his stable sex life. He has no plans to change anything.

The fourth type is the **eligible bachelor**. He is sophisticated, subtle and very well presented. Understanding the needs and wants of his potential partners, he is attentive and regularly gives gifts and compliments. Rather than working with a large number of potential partners, he chooses a small number of his ideal partner type. In this way he can maximise his attentive behaviours, making the potential partners each feel special. When he does finally gain a sexual victory, he continues to woo that partner, knowing that the chase is the hardest part of the relationship, and that the carnal relationship will develop in intensity and regularity as trust builds between him and his chosen partners.

Now, although this model may not be strictly politically correct, it does demonstrate my point. As you were reading about the four types of male, I'm sure you were aware of the traits that you may or may not have noted in your marketing, or the marketing of someone else.

One of the things that the eligible bachelor knows, as do Guerrillas, is that gifts can break the ice, develop a relationship, and show that you are still interested – even after the sale. In fact, the latter reason is perhaps the best reason to give a gift. Your competitors offer gifts to capture prospects, but how many of your competitors continue to give gifts after a prospect becomes a customer? I'll tell you – not many. Differentiate yourself by continuing to provide attention and gifts after the prospect has consented to become a customer.

Does it really work? Yes, it does. One of my clients sent a single rose, costing less than £7, to the personal assistant of the CEO of an existing customer, on her birthday. The CEO saw the gift and asked where it had come from. When the PA told him he simply nodded. However, at the unconscious level he now knew that my client was attentive to a lady who had no decision-making power. During the next meeting with my client he actually said that he wanted to do more business with them, because he was impressed that my client should send such a lovely gift without seeking anything in return. A gift sent without seeking gain actually resulted in nearly £400,000 of extra business. That was a brilliant £7 investment. Gifts are a great Guerrilla Marketing weapon.

Creating profit

I'll make this as simple as I can. Profit is the reason why you are in business. It is the yardstick by which you should measure all of your marketing. It should be the means by which you calculate your successes and failures. It is the reason why you invest, the reason why you employ staff and the reason why you are reading this book.

Marketing is not about building brand awareness. It's about creating profit. There is no point in millions of people recognising your brand if they don't then purchase.

Advertising is not about column inches in the press, or the number of minutes of airtime you get on local or national radio. It's about creating profit.

Marketing is not about being clever. It's about creating profit.

Marketing is not about white space or layout. It's about creating profit.

Marketing is not about brand positioning. It's about creating profit.

Marketing is not about huge investment to capture market share. It's about creating profit.

Marketing is not about expansion. It's about creating profit.

Do you get the idea?

The traits and skills I've highlighted in this chapter are to be found in all exceptional marketers. I'm certain you either possess or are aware of most of them. The ones that you have not yet mastered should be your goal. When you see consistency in your own performance, you'll begin to see consistency in your results, too.

To make success a habit you just need to refuse to accept anything but your best – the Guerrilla way. You have the skill set, the weapons and the know-how. Now you need to apply all that you know. *That* is what will set your performance apart from those of most other marketers. Lots of marketers know how to run a profitable campaign, and they may even have the skill set to do so. The problem is that they lack the constitution to follow through with action.

If you have the will to succeed, you will launch your Guerrilla Marketing attack today.

CHAPTER 9

Act Like a Child

Guerrillas know that modelling excellence and the character traits of successful people is a wonderful way to improve performance. As any parent can testify, we all learn immeasurable amounts from our children. The idea of taking the character traits of a youngster and building them into the behaviour of sales and marketing professionals is not a new one, yet to my mind the full potential has never been realised until now. It's easy to list traits, and I've chosen to expand on that to show you how Guerrillas can actively use what we learn from children.

There are nine traits that I want to present to you, and each is packed full of profits if you manage its application properly.

1. Children are persistent

My son is ten years old. In keeping with the trend among UK youngsters, he loves playing with cards from the *Uh-Gi-Oh!* trading card game. A new range of the cards was recently released in the UK. I knew this not because I'd seen the adverts or received direct marketing materials, but because my son told me about the range three or four times a day. He told me where they could be bought, how much they cost, which decks of cards were his preferred choice, and once when we were shopping in town, he physically took me to the merchandising stand to show me what they looked like.

Surprisingly, at no point did he actually ask me to buy the cards for him. However, the flow of information continued. After a week I felt as though I had an intimate understanding of the cards and the monsters featured on them; indeed, I was even becoming familiar with the battle tactics – yet I had never even touched a single card. Soon, the day of reckoning came. My son asked, 'Dad, if I do some weeding in your garden, could you buy me some *Uh-Gi-Oh!* cards please?' I agreed, and I have no doubt that had I refused, the flow of information would have continued until such time as the purchase was made.

As a marketing model, the strategy applied by my son (whether by intention or good fortune) was sound, and completely consistent with Guerrilla Marketing practice. He gave me an ample supply of free information, maintained a consistent theme, provided me with purchasing instructions and used a number of 'soft steps' before asking for the purchasing decision. When asking for that decision, he even presented a benefit to me first (i.e. my garden would have weeds removed). At no point in time did I give any buying signals, yet he continued his campaign of information presentation – keeping his beloved cards in my mind. Persistence is necessary in any Guerrilla Marketing campaign, as without it prospects and customers may doubt your commitment or simply forget your expertly crafted USP.

2. Children ask questions – lots of questions

If you walked into your doctor's office and said, 'Doctor, I have a pain in ...' and he interrupted you and said, 'Yep, that's fine. Here's your prescription,' would you feel as though you had received the best possible treatment? Obviously not. So why do sales and marketing professionals all over the world do exactly the same thing to their clients? They go into the client's office, and they've already decided what they will sell to that client.

Children are naturally inquisitive and ask questions about everything, often to the point of frustration. Asking questions is important. As we gain answers, we gain knowledge. When we are talking we are learning nothing. Despite what you may have been told, the skill is not in listening – anyone can listen. The skill is in asking questions that show you have been listening. Your questions indicate to any prospect, customer, friend or relative exactly how much of their message you understood and (more importantly) the fact that you created your question as a response to their comments, not that you were simply waiting for them to finish talking so you could have your say.

Questions should make use of the Milton and Meta Models (see page 36), depending on how much vagueness you want to include. Remember, using the Milton Model requires that the listener must associate their own experiences, understanding and background to the question in order to fully comprehend. Conversely, the Meta Model asks a question in a precise and focused manner, leaving no doubt as to the question content.

- **Milton Model** 'Did they all notice a certain change?'

- **Meta Model** 'Did Brian, Michael and Henry notice the 15 per cent increase in revenue during April?'

The more skilful you become in constructing and delivering questions, the more information will be given to you freely. The knock-on effect is that you will be better able to create marketing materials and business proposals that satisfy the requirements of your prospects.

3. Children refuse to be restricted by the realities of others

I'm a motor-sport fan. In fact, just a few years back I was actively racing unlimited V8 cars in British Stock Car Association (BRISCA) Formula One. Now I simply enjoy watching and attend as many meetings as I can find time to visit.

There was one occasion when I had returned from an extended business trip. For 30 days I had been travelling throughout Russia, the US, South Africa and northern Europe. In an entire calendar month, I had spent only five nights in my own bed. On my first weekend back I decided to take my son to see some BRISCA racing, and my friends John and Karen came too.

On the way, we became caught in heavy traffic. To pass the time, my son (who was five at the time) suggested a game of 'I Spy'. I'd played with him many times before, so suggested, 'I have to concentrate on driving, but John and Karen will play with you.' John threw a vicious glare my way, and then agreed.

My son began, 'I spy with my little eye something beginning with 'S'.' The guesses came fast and furious, but each was met with, 'No.' Five minutes into the game I was very glad I'd chosen to side-step personal involvement. John's frustration was clear, and Karen had given up.

Ten minutes into the game and it had become a personal challenge for John. He was not going to be beaten by a five-year-old child. 'Sky', 'seagull' and 'sandwiches' were all dismissed as incorrect.

After 15 minutes John finally admitted defeat. Proudly realising his victory, my son announced, 'South Africa.'

'You can't see South Africa,' John complained.

'Why not?' the child questioned, 'My dad did.'

This story clearly presents an uncomfortable truth for many marketers. No matter how many years experience you have, or how many qualifications you have, your model of the world is personal to you, and not necessarily to anyone else. My son felt that his using

'South Africa' during the game was fine, yet John felt that the rules had been violated. So who was right? They both were. No one can tell you that your model is wrong, because no one else can completely experience all elements of your model.

The other side of this argument is that when a prospect or client describes an issue, problem or belief, they may not realise that their model is not the only possible model. Asking someone, or leading someone, to think outside of their usual model is a wonderful technique for opening new opportunities. During Guerrilla Marketing 'practitioner' training courses we teach delegates how to use this very technique to open new avenues of dialogue. Let's suppose that during a meeting a prospect has offered the objection, 'We don't outsource training.' Traditional sales or marketing training would require that you ask, 'Why not?' As Guerrillas we ask, 'What would happen if you did?' The immediate effect is that the prospect absolutely must consider an option outside of their present model.

In the majority of cases the prospect will answer, 'Well, we just don't.' This doesn't answer your wonderfully crafted question, so you repeat the question – but speak more slowly, placing an emphasis on every word.

In many cases the prospect will still resist and may answer, 'It's company policy,' or 'We just never do.' Once again you insist upon an answer, and a movement from their present model, by repeating your question even more slowly than before. Maintain this repetition strategy until the prospect demonstrates that they have considered an option outside of their current model. This will often manifest itself by way of a rather sheepish, 'I suppose we would get a new perspective,' or a reluctant, 'I can see that it might introduce some skills that we don't have in-house.' By simply leading the prospect to a different model of reality, that prospect has now accepted that there is another version of reality. They may not be persuaded by this alone, but accepting that there is another reality opens the floodgates for your persuasive suggestions, as at the unconscious level they will always know that your version of reality might just be right.

Traditional sales and marketing training suggests that if a

prospect or client offers the objection, 'It's too expensive,' then the preferred response should be, 'It's too expensive compared to what?' Guerrillas know that this is no longer the best response. In fact, it is a weak response for one very important reason – you are accepting and confirming that the prospect's belief is valid. We now know that the only way to effectively persuade anyone, in the long term, is to have them question their own beliefs – not to impose your beliefs upon them. So to reinforce the prospect's belief by asking for a comparison is simply not going to help you persuade anyone.

A better response – the Guerrilla response – might be, 'What makes you say that?' This uncomplicated question does three things, it:

1. Requires that the prospect explores and questions their decision.

2. Requires that the prospect qualify their objection to you by describing the decision-making strategy used (i.e. through verbal behaviour).

3. Allows you an insight into the prospect's decision-making strategies through non-verbal behaviour, such as eye-access cues and other physiology.

When responding to objections and queries, Guerrillas ask questions that require the speaker to revisit the decision-making strategy, by considering another version of reality. We ask children to do it all the time. For example:

- When a child asks for some chocolate, we might ask, 'Wouldn't you rather eat some fruit?'

- If a child crosses a road without first looking, we may ask, 'What would have happened if a car had been coming along the road?'

These are examples that we use without even thinking about it – consciously. Try to use this technique in your everyday business life and watch the results. You'll amaze yourself, and wonder why you never tried it before.

4. Children have very active imaginations

Throughout their young lives, we enthusiastically encourage the imaginations of our children. Where an adult sees a cardboard box, a child sees a spaceship worth hours of play. Some children play for hours with imaginary friends. However, when we become adults, some of us allow our imaginations to die off. Or do we?

One of the traits we regularly see in successful people is that they are imaginative in the way they address problems and issues that may stall others.

This next statement is very important – really important. If you need to write it down to remember, go and get a pen and paper now. It really is that important.

You can be just as imaginative as anyone else on Earth.

Imagination has nothing to do with intelligence, stress, upbringing, class or culture. Imagination is simply our ability to visualise something. Remember the blue elephant at the beginning of this book (see page 6)? That was your imagination at work. Each and every one of us has natural creative abilities. Some people have better developed abilities than others, and some have more discipline in managing their own mind. This is the factor that controls how you direct your imagination.

Nikola Tesla was one of the greatest inventors in history. He was responsible for many inventions that are still around today, including hydroelectric power stations, AC electricity, the speedometer, fluorescent bulbs and radio.

Tesla had an exceptionally developed ability to visualise his ideas. However, he not only could visualise simple objects and images, but also had the ability to manage animation and construction in his mind. Once, he designed a prototype motor in his mind, while an identical motor was built elsewhere. He imagined how the motor would operate over a period of time, and was able to accurately predict which moving parts would wear, and to what degree. When the identical real motor was disassembled, his predictions were accurate to thousandths of an inch.

Was Tesla more intelligent than everyone else? No, not necessarily. He was clearly very intelligent and well educated, but most importantly he had mastered his own mind. His visualisation skills (his ability to imagine) are skills that anyone can possess, improve and master.

So what use is a well-developed imagination to Guerrilla Marketers? In short, a good imagination can help you solve problems. There is a simple method that has been developed and shown to give great results. This method has been built upon the modelling of many successful sales and marketing professionals, and may at first reading seem too simple. The fact is that its simplicity is the reason why it is not utilised more. Many business professionals believe it is beneath them to try it, and for that very reason I urge you to do so.

Having read the previous chapters in this book, you now know that the unconscious mind has the entirety of your memories, logic, experiences and emotions to call upon to make decisions. You also know that the unconscious mind does not always fully share this resource with the conscious mind. Use your imagination to address a problem in these three simple steps:

1. Ask yourself a direct question, posed in a positive manner, for example 'What must I do to get money today?'

2. Keep asking the question until you get an answer.

3. Do not accept anything except the answer to your question.

This method truly works. Until you try it you will not understand how good it feels to use it, and get results. The reason why it works is because the more you ask yourself the same question and reject irrelevant answers, the more resource the unconscious mind allocates, as it recognises the importance in reaching an answer. The more ruthless you are in accepting only the required response, the more resources the unconscious mind assigns.

Children do it, Tesla did it – and you can do it now.

5. Children rarely accept 'no' as a final answer

Young children have not typically polished their questioning skills, but the majority of children are relentless with whatever task is at hand. If a child wants something badly enough, they will ask for it many times over. Some children simply pose the same question in a number of different ways. It is important to note, though, that children almost never give up after just one 'no'.

The Chartered Institute of Purchasing and Supply conducted a study which offered some results that are very significant for sales and marketing professionals. They found that 92 per cent of sales and marketing professionals stop presenting their product or service to a client after being told 'no' four times. They also found that 73 per cent of buyers give the 'no' message five times (or more) before buying.

Stop and think about that.

This means that 8 per cent of sales and marketing professionals are marketing to 73 per cent of the market, because everyone else has given up. Have you given up after hearing 'no' four times? Consider another implication of these statistics: 92 per cent of all sales and marketing professionals are marketing to just 27 per cent of the available market.

Children believe that 'no' means 'maybe' and that often 'maybe' means 'yes'.

Guerrillas know that if the qualification process has been completed properly, then 'no' usually means 'not yet'. Plenty of easy soft steps, provision of free information and commitment to the marketing plan will move the client or prospect swiftly to a 'yes, please'.

6. Children enjoy learning

John Stuart Mill once wrote, 'He who knows only his own side of the argument, knows little of that.' In sales, marketing, training, education and parenting, there are two words that do more damage than good, yet I hear them in almost every consultancy I attend and every training session I facilitate. The words? 'I know'.

When we host training seminars we absolutely know that if the attendees make use of the skills, strategies and methods that we present to them, then they will profit. We also know that statistics have repeatedly shown that only 5 to 10 per cent of training seminar attendees will act upon training material in the long term. Why? The larger part of the mind of the typical salesman or marketer is controlled by ego. Guerrillas know that ego has no place in any marketing campaign because an ego is built upon a single reality, and as we have already discussed, Guerrillas understand that there are always multiple realities.

Any consultant feels frustrated when time is spent studying an organisation, the options available to the client are considered, a proposal document is authored and then the client does nothing. The same is true of trainers. Many ask themselves, 'Why are these people here, when only 5 to 10 per cent will act on this training material?'

There is a huge difference between children and the typical sales or marketing professional, when considering learning. Children love to absorb new information. Sights, sounds, feelings and stories excite children. At the opposite end of the spectrum are the sales or marketing professionals who have been in business for ten or fifteen years. At the unconscious level, they hate the idea that someone can present something not already known to them. How can they be taught, when they've been successful for ten years? There lies the reason why so many organisations stagnate.

Military personnel, doctors, surgeons, lawyers, accountants and teachers all receive regular training updates – so why is sales and marketing training 'fudged'? It is a sad fact that the majority of marketing professionals in business today received training with material that was written 20 or 30 years ago, and have not updated their training since. Do you think industry has changed over the past 30 years? I certainly do.

Guerrillas enjoy learning. The Guerrilla Marketing Association hosts free weekly training sessions for its members to ensure that all Guerrilla Marketing practitioners are using current methods and skills. The training sessions are hosted by the marketing industry's leaders, so the information is always the best available.

The day you honestly believe you don't need any further training is the day your ego has finally taken control of your mind – and ego doesn't create profit.

7. Children love to be the first to talk about something new

How many times have you heard a child say, 'I know something you don't know,' or open a conversation with, 'You'll never guess what'? Now consider how many times you've heard someone accused of 'gossip'. It is a human character trait ingrained in each and every one of us – we love to be the first to introduce news.

Earlier in this book (see page 86), I discussed how it is possible to create a competitive advantage by simply detailing something you already do in everyday business. It may even be the case that some of your competitors do exactly the same thing, but by being the first to tell everyone that you do it, the competitive advantage becomes yours – as very few competitors will want to be a 'me too'.

Examine your own business today. Don't be shy. Find something that is part of your normal business operations, but may amaze your prospects. Remember, your model of the world (and your business) is not the only model. Something that you consider boring, mundane or expected may be exactly what your prospects value most. Whatever you decide to use, be the first to do so. Examples might be:

- All products are picked and packed by hand.

- All our consultants are licensed Guerrilla Marketing practitioners.

- All enquiries receive a response within 24 hours.

- Our software applications are built upon Microsoft technology.

Each of these could be a competitive advantage if positioned well in the right industry. Each will also probably be employed by some of your competitors, but because you're the first to offer it as a competitive advantage, the industry will accept it as your competitive advantage.

8. Children try to make everything fun

Ask yourself something right now, and be completely honest. When you get up each morning, do you do so because you're excited about starting on your work, or because you have to use the bathroom before your partner? Do you bounce out of bed wondering, 'What cool things can I do today?' or do you say to yourself, 'Oh no! It's morning already.'

Children have the ability to find fun in the most unusual circumstances. I remember once I was driving with my son across Malta. The weather was glorious and the scenery was amazing. Without any great thought, and at my son's suggestion, soon we were playing 'Who can see the most yellow hats?' We played this game for more than 30 minutes.

So at what point in our life do we lose the ability to find fun in anything? We don't. If anyone tells you that we necessarily do, kick them. Kick them and laugh. You should find that fun.

Without doubt, if you enjoy an activity, you are more likely to succeed and excel in it. Olympic athletes love what they do. Professional sportsmen and women believe they are the luckiest people on Earth. Successful artists believe they are leading the ideal life. Guerrillas know that they are lucky to understand the strategies, methods and weapons that will make them successful. Guerrillas also know that making work fun can make success a habit.

So how do we make work fun? There are three simple ways:

1. Surround yourself with people that you enjoy spending time with.

2. Throughout the day, keep asking yourself, 'How can I have more fun?' and 'How can I make this more enjoyable?'

3. When you see success, reward yourself (this can be real fun).

Apply these three easy steps and not only will your life become more fun, but also the quality of your life will improve, because your stress levels will drop and you will therefore be more relaxed both at home and at work.

9. Children talk until they believe they're understood

Parents know that this trait is absolutely found in all children. It is not unusual for children to repeat themselves many times to ensure that the intended message is understood. There lies one of the most misunderstood rules of communication. Traditional marketing teaches that your message should be clear for all to understand. Guerrilla Marketing supports this belief, but adds, 'The message is whatever communication is understood by the receiver.'

Communication is a five-stage process:

1. The speaker explores his requirements and creates a message.

2. The speaker transmits the message.

3. The message is received.

4. The receiver interprets the surface structure of the message.

5. The receiver goes through derivation processes to interpret the deep structure of the message.

If any stage of this communication process is flawed in any way, the message will be interpreted as incomplete, or the derivation processes will develop a message other than that intended. By creating rapport with the receiver before transmitting a message, the likelihood that the message will be received as intended is hugely increased.

It is quite usual for a child to ask for something three or four times, even when told 'yes'. This is an inexperienced communicator's way of ensuring that all five stages of the communication process have been completed correctly. Funnily enough, it is also a trait shown by poor sales and marketing professionals. A study conducted by Guerrilla Marketing UK in 2003 showed that 74 per cent of buyers said that they would have purchased earlier if they had been asked. Instead, many sales and marketing executives feel they need to conduct their rehearsed presentation, regardless of any attempt at interaction.

Guerrillas add a sixth stage

A better means of establishing that the communication process has passed precisely, and a method used by experienced Guerrillas, is to add a sixth stage to the communication process. This is done by asking a question of the receiver, or compelling the receiver to clearly display an understanding of the original message and its implication in the context in which it was used. Typically, this is actioned through a 'call to action'. This in itself is not a new marketing strategy. However, we now know that if you build rapport early enough in copy, presentations and meetings, then you can request the 'call to action' much earlier than ever thought possible.

So what is the strategy that shortens the sales cycle in this way? Actually, we've already covered it earlier (see page 46). The use of 'undeniable truths' builds rapport quickly. When used properly, alongside the other language patterns discussed in previous chapters (see for example page 35), you will find that you can request commitments, actions and promises of your prospects and clients far ahead of what would be considered usual. Why? Because you display an understanding of your clients, and require that they show an understanding of your messages. This is communication excellence – the Guerrilla way.

Is there a better way to recognise that you have been understood than to receive the order?

New Weapons for Your Arsenal

GUERRILLA MARKETING IS BUILT upon the belief that combinations of marketing weapons are the routes to profitable success. In previous books I have listed 100 Guerrilla Marketing weapons, and it's now time to present them to you again, before I extend that list.

100 Guerrilla Marketing weapons

1. Marketing plan
2. Marketing calendar
3. Niche/positioning
4. Name of company
5. Identity
6. Logo
7. Theme
8. Stationery
9. Business card
10. Signs inside

11. Signs outside
12. Hours of operation
13. Days of operation
14. Window display
15. Flexibility
16. Word-of-mouth
17. Community involvement
18. Barter
19. Club/Association memberships
20. Partial payment plans
21. Cause-related marketing
22. Telephone manner
23. Toll free phone number
24. Free consultations
25. Free seminars and clinics
26. Free demonstrations
27. Free samples
28. Giver vs taker stance
29. Fusion marketing
30. Marketing on telephone hold
31. Success stories
32. Employee attire
33. Service
34. Follow-up
35. Yourself and your employees
36. Gifts and ad specialities
37. Catalogue
38. Yellow Pages ads
39. Column in a publication
40. Article in a publication
41. Speaker at any club

42. Newsletter
43. All your audiences
44. Benefits list
45. Computer
46. Selection
47. Contact time with customer
48. How you say hello/goodbye
49. Public relations
50. Media contacts
51. Neatness
52. Referral programme
53. Sharing with peers
54. Guarantee
55. Telemarketing
56. Gift certificates
57. Brochures
58. Electronic brochures
59. Location
60. Advertising
61. Sales training
62. Networking
63. Quality
64. Reprints and blow-ups
65. Flipcharts
66. Opportunities to upgrade
67. Contests/sweepstakes
68. Online marketing
69. Classified advertising
70. Newspaper ads
71. Magazine ads
72. Radio spots

73. TV spots
74. Infomercials
75. Movie ads
76. Direct mail letters
77. Direct mail postcards
78. Postcard decks
79. Posters
80. Fax-on-demand
81. Special events
82. Show display
83. Audio-visual aids
84. Spare time
85. Prospect mailing lists
86. Research studies
87. Competitive advantages
88. Marketing insight
89. Travel
90. Testimonials
91. Reputation
92. Enthusiasm & passion
93. Credibility
94. Spying on yourself and others
95. Being easy to do business with
96. Brand name awareness
97. Designated guerrilla
98. Customer mailing list
99. Competitiveness
100. Satisfied customers

I've introduced some terrific new methods, great new strategies and a collection of innovative Guerrilla Marketing weapons in this

book. There are 25 new methods in total, and each is described suc-
cinctly below. Some have already been discussed, and in these cases
I provide references to the additional material provided earlier.

1. Focus on the unconscious mind

I hope that by now you are fully convinced that you need to persuade the unconscious mind, rather than focus on the conscious
mind. I've presented many reasons for this, and the most important
reason is that the unconscious mind actually makes all decisions.
Sometimes it shares its decision with the conscious awareness, and
sometimes it chooses not to.

When you seek to influence a large, multinational organisation,
would you rather have a meeting with the CEO or with one of his
20 area managers? The CEO has more information and more
resources available to him than the area manager does. As a result,
the CEO will (in most cases) make a better-informed decision.

The same is true of the unconscious mind. It has more resources
available to it, works more quickly and has high-speed access to the
huge database of experiences known as memory. As a result it typically makes the best decision that can be made with the data available.

Directing your marketing at the unconscious minds of your
prospects is the newest and most exciting of the Guerrilla Marketing weapons. Most traditional marketers do not understand this
weapon, and even fewer know how to use it. As such, it's even more
powerful in your arsenal – but only if you use it!

2. Congruence

I mentioned this briefly in Chapter 7 (see page 94), and it is an
essential weapon – in fact only recently have I come to fully understand how essential it actually is. Now we have a better understanding of its application, we truly understand its power. Without

congruence in your marketing activity, your prospects will take much longer to accept and trust your message. The longer the acceptance takes, the more it costs you – and that means a reduction in your profits. It is critical that you identify with the true meaning of congruence in Guerrilla Marketing.

Congruence is, at the most basic level, maintaining a consistent and predictable identity in everything that you do. If your corporate identity is that of a hi-tech company, and that is accepted as your identity by the market, then every single marketing activity should support this identity. You should use hi-tech methods and Guerrilla Marketing weapons. To use traditional or low-tech methods would be incongruent, and would confuse the market, and a confused prospect is not ready to purchase. Ensure that congruence is applied to your whole organisation, from the way the phones are answered and the appearance of your direct mailings, to the way your sales teams present your benefits. Everything should support your identity.

3. Representational systems

I did not create this weapon, and I would not claim to have done so. Representational systems were identified and developed by Dr Richard Bandler and Dr John Grinder – the creators of NLP. As such, representational systems have been in use for more than 30 years. To effectively market in the modern world, you need to understand how this weapon works. The average person is exposed to 30,000 marketing messages a day, so to make yours stand out you need to optimise your communications expertise.

If your message is more focused and presented in a manner that is naturally attractive at the unconscious level, it will shine through the surplus of traditional marketing messages. We covered representational systems in depth in earlier chapters (see for example pages 22–25), so take some time to review the material. Investing some time now will save you investing your money in poor marketing at a later date.

4. Language patterns

This is one of the most exciting new Guerrilla Marketing weapons. It is actually a collection of four weapons (presuppositions, deletions, ambiguities and embedded commands), but for our purposes I've chosen to group them all under one weapon heading. The reason why this is such an exciting weapon is because there are very few people who truly know how to use it at all, and an even smaller group of marketers who have any understanding of the possible applications.

The weapon has been used profitably in some marketing campaigns completely by accident. However, in Guerrilla Marketing everything we do is intentional, so you really do need to learn how to use language patterns to your advantage. In Chapter 3 (see page 36) I explained how to use language patterns, and provided some examples, too. Use these examples as templates for your own creations. The more you practise constructing persuasive language patterns, the easier they will become for you. Remember, the unconscious mind allocates more resources to learn skills that it considers important, and the more you practise a skill, the quicker the unconscious mind recognises the importance of that skill. Start now. Go to Chapter 3 right away and pick out the examples that you feel you can adapt to your needs today. Language patterns will improve your copy immediately, so the sooner you apply this weapon the better.

5. Risk reversal

Earlier on I presented the results of a research study that showed that 'confidence in the business' is one of the major reasons why purchasers choose whether to buy from you, or from your competitors. Congruence is an excellent way to help build confidence, as is consistency in your marketing message. When people say 'confidence in the business' what they actually mean is 'low risk in my decision'. This is especially true in business-to-business (B2B) markets, as a bad decision can lose you your job. Consumers will not lose their jobs through a bad decision, but no one likes to make a bad decision, so if you can reduce the risk in the purchasing decision then you have already made it easier for the purchaser to say 'yes'.

There are a number of ways in which you can reduce the risk for prospects and customers. Guarantees, warranties, pilot studies, samples, trial periods and deferred payment schemes are all weapons that come under the heading 'risk reversal'. Each of these methods reduces risk for the purchaser, by shifting the risk over to you. This may sound like a foolish thing to do until you consider the perceived benefits for the purchaser:

1. You obviously have great belief in your product.

2. Your marketing messages must be true, to take the financial risk of a guarantee that could result in a refund.

3. You must want the purchaser to be happy in the long term.

4. You must be an established organisation to offer a guarantee.

5. You trust the purchaser to be honest.

Each of these reasons may or may not be true – it doesn't matter. The perception to the purchaser is what matters, and by shifting the risk from the purchaser to you, you make the purchasing decision easier.

This next statement may confuse, bemuse or just plain baffle you. Make your guarantee unconditional and lifetime in length.

Anyone can offer a 14-day guarantee. Some will offer a 30-day or 90-day guarantee. Make your guarantee a lifetime guarantee. Obviously, there are some time-sensitive products this cannot apply to. (I can't imagine TV manufacturers offering lifetime guarantees.) However, even in these instances, you should aim to make your guarantee longer than those of your competition. In the UK, Daewoo was the first car manufacturer to offer a three-year guarantee on new cars, and they captured a huge market share. Suddenly, all the other manufacturers were extending their guarantees to three years, too.

When marketing products and services that are not time sensitive, extend your guarantee beyond all known offers. Make yours a 'Better than lifetime, refund for whatever reason you like, whenever you like' guarantee. It will amaze you, but you will get almost no refund requests! You, like me three years ago, will probably feel that the market is full of people just waiting to take advantage of your good nature – and your guarantee. Having tested this theory myself, and having tested it with 60 or more of my own clients, I can tell you that if a refund is not sought in the first 30 days, it is very rarely requested. Trust the quality of your products and services, and have faith in humanity. Not everyone is trying to cheat everyone else. Reverse the risk for your prospects and customers and watch your profits increase.

6. Headlines

From reading Chapter 6 (see page 83) you'll know that headlines are almost an obsession for me, now I've realised their power. If you have ten hours to write a sales letter, spend nine hours on the headline. Your headline must capture the attention of the reader, as if it does not then your wonderfully crafted copy will be wasted. I won't repeat the messages in Chapter 6 here, so just be aware of three things:

1. Closed questions do not usually perform well in a headline. They do not require any interaction from the reader. Use open questions that necessitate interaction through derivation.

2. Intrigue is irresistible to most people, so intrigue people.

3. If a publication uses one type of headline more than twice, it's because it works. Model that headline and craft your own based upon its structure. (Why reinvent the wheel, right?)

Headlines are a required component in the make-up of almost all sales and marketing letters. Experiment and test. When you have a headline that works well, keep testing variations of that headline. Always seek improvement, and never stop testing.

7. Velocity

Now, speed is something that everyone understands. Velocity is slightly different, and I've included it because I really like the dictionary definition. In the Concise Oxford English Dictionary the word 'velocity' is defined as 'the rate of speed of action'. This is perfect for Guerrilla Marketing, as all weapons, theories, strategies and techniques are powerless without action – and velocity focuses on action.

Velocity is naturally incorporated into Guerrilla Marketing, by virtue of the fact that Guerrilla organisations are very proactive, react more quickly than traditional organisations and are always seeking new ways to gain an advantage utilising time, effort and imagination, instead of a huge marketing budget – which you probably don't have anyway.

To wholly apply velocity to your marketing, you need to realise that your ability to act more quickly than large blue-chip companies is a competitive advantage. Where multinational companies may need to document procedural changes, and possibly even minute such changes in monthly board meetings, Guerrilla organisations document the changes and action them at the earliest practicable time – once testing has shown a profitable motivation for the changes.

Where traditional organisations refuse to move quickly, because 'that's not the way we do business', Guerrilla organisations know that moving quickly is often the most profitable way to do business.

Who was the second man to run the four-minute mile? Who was the second man to break the sound barrier? Who was the second man to climb Mount Everest? There is a benefit in being first!

Do not risk your corporate identity, or indeed profitable marketing campaigns, to move quickly. Congruence is important in everything you do. However, do not believe the myth that you have to run your business the same way as everyone else does. Move quickly, decisively and profitably.

8. The Golden Ratio

I explained the Golden Ratio sufficiently in Chapter 6 (see page 78). Review the material in depth. Although not complex, it is an advanced, detailed weapon.

The Golden Ratio is a little-known and often misunderstood weapon. As a Guerrilla with true understanding of its potential and application requirements, you have a mighty new arrow in your quiver.

9. P.S.

I introduced this in Chapter 6 (see page 83). If you've ever read a sales letter all the way through, the chances are it had a P.S. *Reader's Digest, Encyclopaedia Britannica*, and hundreds of others have used a P.S. at the end of their sales letters for many years. The reason is performance based – a good P.S. adds value to your letter.

I've personally tested letters with a P.S. and letters without a P.S., and without exception the letters with a P.S. brought more responses across every single industry.

A word of warning. In this book I have introduced some language patterns designed for influencing your prospects and customers. Please remember when creating your P.S. that persuasive language patterns should not be placed in the P.S. This is because we need rapport with the reader for maximum persuasive ability, and since the P.S. is usually the first part of the letter to be read in full, the letter has not built rapport with the reader before they read the P.S. As a result the language pattern is wasted, and may damage the intended covert delivery of forthcoming language patterns.

The P.S. is a wonderful Guerrilla Marketing weapon, but only when used properly. Use yours to set the tone for your letter.

10. Live chat interaction

There are now millions of people who use live chat applications online. This is a weapon that Guerrillas have embraced, and indeed many of our Guerrilla Marketing sites (including mine) now make use of interactive chat software.

Imagine this scenario; you visit a website and begin to look around. Suddenly a pop-up chat window appears, and a message from 'client services' says, 'I notice you've been looking through our portfolio. Would you like to see our most recent case study?' You respond, and very quickly realise that you are talking to a real person, not a robot. Within seconds you are being shown around the website. This is not simply a story. This is a reality for some websites.

The cost of this technology? Less than £1 per day! (And it can actually be free if you use your Guerrilla guile and become an affiliate or reseller, too.) This is a very powerful Guerrilla Marketing weapon because it can reduce the purchasing decision time. Most websites are simply shop windows, displaying some benefits, and providing basic information and some contact details. Guerrillas know that customer interaction is the way to enhance your website.

Clients who need help finding information can now be helped immediately, in real time. Prospects who need to ask a question can get instant gratification, rather than sending an email and waiting for someone to respond. This weapon is fantastic. It employs velocity, interaction, risk reduction, convenience and great customer service. Most website visitors seek all these.

11. Avatars

This is one of the most state-of-the-moment weapons to be added to the Guerrilla arsenal. An avatar is a virtual character on a website, often capable of speech. Recently, the trend has been to have an avatar in the role of website guide or customer service personnel. On my own website, I have an avatar called Cassie. She wears a smart camouflage uniform, in keeping with the recognised Guerrilla Marketing meme (memes are covered on page 74), and has been programmed to smile before answering any questions.

Cassie welcomes visitors to the website and hosts the Q&A page. This means that when visitors click on a question, instead of reading a page of detailed copy, Cassie smiles and responds in soft tones with perfect grammar. The feedback I've received has been excellent. Visitors both male and female love Cassie.

This is only one application for an avatar. It is perfectly possible to add an artificial intelligence engine, so the avatar can respond to freeform questions with intelligent and relevant answers. The wave of the future? Today, avatars still have an innovation attraction. As they become more common, they may lose the novelty value, but as avatar technology advances I believe this weapon will become more powerful and useful. Watch this space.

12. Modelling excellence

Without any doubt whatsoever, this weapon will be the most profitable one you will ever discover, yet I fear that it will remain the most underused weapon in the Guerrilla Marketing arsenal.

As already described earlier (see page 113), modelling involves observing and detailing the successful processes that enable an exceptional performance. In Guerrilla Marketing we use modelling to discover and then recreate excellence. For example, if someone shows exceptional expertise in direct mail applications, wouldn't it be great to model that expertise and implant it in yourself, or others? Well, now you can. The same is true of any chosen performance, in any compliant person. If someone can do something better than you, find out how they do it. Do you know people who are more successful in business than you? Model them. If you know people who are better at closing business than you – model them. If you see any performance in others that you desire in yourself, ask them if they will allow you to model them. Elicit their strategies and embrace them for yourself.

Some of the most successful business professionals on Earth have used this method. So why not model them? Just a thought.

13. Positive outcome stance

This weapon is very important for two reasons; firstly, it will differentiate you from the large percentage of your competition. Secondly, it is more professional and responsible than traditional methods.

Earlier on (see page 53) I discussed how the schools of thought in traditional sales and marketing circles describe a method whereby you should identify a pain that your prospect or customer presently has, build and expand upon that pain, and then offer a solution – your solution. In effect, this method causes the prospect or customer enough discomfort to make the solution seem a desirable outcome.

In Guerrilla Marketing we always seek to build long-term relationships with our prospects and customers. We also seek to make relationships as easy and pleasant for both parties as we can manage. This raises a question about the 'pain' method used by traditional marketing organisations – why would you want your prospects or clients to feel bad?

The 'pain' method is an alternative to creative, professional and responsible marketing. If you need to create pain in your prospects and customers to motivate them to buy your product or service, you need to review your benefits and competitive advantage.

Guerrillas know that positive outcomes are the quickest way to motivate the purchasing decision. By making your prospects and customers feel great about the purchasing decision, you remove the risk of buyer's remorse. A positive outcome stance should be sought in all your marketing activity.

14. Accepting multiple currencies

This weapon supports a key belief for Guerrillas everywhere; your business should be run for the convenience of your clients, not you. If your website doesn't accept payment in pounds, dollars, euros and yen you are losing business.

Some banks limit online credit card payments to the currency of the country where the card owner resides. For instance, some UK debit and credit cards cannot pay in any currency except British pounds. Conversely, some Russian cards can only pay in roubles or dollars – so your British website is alienating a percentage of the Russian nation. Do you honestly want to miss out on that many prospects?

Start your research today. I think you'll be pleasantly surprised. It costs very little to enable additional currencies for most eCommerce applications, and for many others it is a free function.

15. Business automation software

This is a weapon that should be used by every business. Business automation software can save you huge amounts of time, by managing your newsletters, auto responders, email inbox, delivery of documents and customer service. In some cases, it can even manage the creation of invoices and payment of your own bills. These are jobs that you no longer need to do.

Technology is a great thing. If you are techno-phobic, go and see a techno-shrink. The technology involved in business automation software is becoming more advanced on a weekly or monthly basis, yet is very simple to put into operation. Applying this weapon will give you more time to spend on important tasks – like your marketing.

16. Taxi advertising

This is a simple yet very effective means of marketing. You can place advertisements on the seat backs, the receipts and even the exterior of a taxicab at very low cost. Better still, one of my clients has just launched a marketing system that utilises a 15-inch TFT monitor in the rear of the taxi, running 30-second TV quality advertisements for the passengers. That's direct marketing to a captive audience. The monitor is directly linked to the taxi meter, so the advertisements are only running when there are passengers in the taxi. For less than the cost of a full-page advertisement in a typical industry publication, you could be running your 30-second advertisement, four times an hour and 24 hours per day, on the screens of 3,000 taxi cabs across the UK. That type of exposure, at low cost, is the Guerrilla Marketing way!

17. Customer feedback committees

This weapon is hardly used at all, yet it offers many benefits to competent Guerrillas. The model is simple. You ask a group of your top clients to come to your offices once a month to sit on the customer feedback committee. The committee is then asked to determine and document what your organisation does well, what it does badly and what it would like to see changed. This has many benefits for you and the members of the committee:

1. You discover what your clients *really* think about your organisation (which enables you to better identify your identity).

2. You are seen as directly addressing your clients' complaints.

3. Your business model can be built around the true needs of the market. Remember that 20 per cent of your client base will provide 80 per cent of the revenue, so if you can directly involve that 20 per cent in your committee they will remain loyal clients.

4. Clients that believe their opinions are being considered are very unlikely to migrate to your competition.

5. When your clients are given the opportunity to exchange stories and experiences with other clients, they are more likely to be completely honest with you.

These are just five of the many reasons you should consider this weapon. Maybe for your organisation holding monthly meetings would be too often, or not often enough. Ask your clients what they think, and set up your committee as soon as you can. Within minutes of the first meeting closing, you will have a better understanding of how your organisation can better serve your prospects and customers, which in turn will mean more profit for you.

18. Virtual office

Guerrillas know that your business should be run for the convenience of your prospects and customers, not your own. The Internet has effectively reduced all international boundaries for business, so you need to be open 24/7. Obviously, sometimes you cannot be in the office, and traditionally when we can't be in the office we leave an answer phone machine to take messages.

Ask yourself this: how many times has someone left a message saying, 'Hi, I'd like to place an order. My name is Mr Smith and my credit card number is....'? It is a fact that no one likes leaving messages on voicemail or answer phone. Think about it. The caller has called you at that time because they wanted to speak to you.

There are now a number of companies who offer a 'virtual office' package. When your office is closed, you divert your telephones to an agreed number. When anyone calls your number, the call is answered in your company name by a real person (who is actually an employee of the virtual office company). This person explains that you are not in the office, and offers to take a message or process the caller's order. When the call is completed you are sent an email, SMS text message or message to a pager detailing the caller's identity and the result of the call. A service such as this costs less than £1 per day. For such a tiny investment you will be guaranteed to never miss a call, or more importantly an order, ever again. There are no reasons why you should not consider this weapon for your organisation.

19. Upgrades and add-ons

You should work on making this weapon second nature for your staff, and include it in all sales and marketing procedures. As already discussed (see page 13), 34 per cent of your existing customers will order from you again if you offer them something similar, or related. By the time they are placing the order, they have already made the purchasing decision and established in their own mind that their reasons to buy are sound. Therefore why not offer an additional or complimentary item at the time of ordering?

If you only have one product or service that you presently offer, consider offering a premium and a 'lite' version. Then when customers place the order for the 'lite' version, you can offer the upgrade to the premium version. If you have more than one product, consider bundling multiple items together. Alternatively, you could add an additional product free of charge – as an unexpected bonus. Don't detail the bonus before the purchase, but after. It adds real value to the add-on. Great add-ons include ebooks, subscriptions to newsletters and any other information products with high-value information. High value, low cost: that's the mark of a true Guerrilla Marketing weapon.

20. Anchors and triggers

This weapon may be considered a language pattern of sorts, but it is unlike the other language patterns that I've presented. To fully understand this weapon you need to read Chapter 6 (see page 87). In order to use anchors and triggers you must appreciate the conditions that need to be in place for an anchor to be suitably set, and for a trigger to be accurately activated. This is a hugely powerful weapon, and it is essential that you realise how destructive it can be for your marketing if you don't use it correctly. Use it with a balance of caution, energy and aggression.

21. Inoculation

This weapon is not my creation, but the brain child of Dr Richard Bandler. He asked a probing question, 'When you know you are at risk from a disease, you get inoculated. You also know what objections you are going to receive time after time, so why not inoculate against those objections?' That great question created the inoculation that we now use in modern Guerrilla Marketing.

Earlier on (see page 63) I explained inoculation in more detail, and gave you some examples of how it can be used. Refresh your mind with those examples now, and add this weapon to your arsenal today.

22. SMS text messaging

Providing you do not abuse this weapon, it will enable you to market where few others dare – and it will build closer relationships with your clients.

On practically every business card you are given, you will find a mobile telephone number. You may use it to call the prospect or customer, but how often do you use it for SMS text messaging?

Your competition is already using email, telephone calls, letters and marketing mail shots in an attempt to capture your clients. So what can you do that is different?

Smart Guerrillas embrace technology and business automation wherever possible. There is now the software available to send an SMS text message to multiple mobile phones at the press of a button, and I particularly like this weapon because it is so personal.

Research the software options. Just imagine how pleasantly surprised your clients would be to receive a text message to their mobile phone, 'Hi, John. I want to let you know that we've just posted a case study on our website that directly relates to your business. Take a look. Warm regards. Jay.'

Personalisation of each text message only requires that you have a database with the clients' names and mobile numbers. Furthermore, since a text message costs so little to send, this is actually a less expensive method than sending a letter. Admittedly an email is even less expensive, but emails are no longer regarded as personal or particularly attentive. We all receive so many commercial emails that we have become desensitised to any personalisation. However, a personalised message delivered to the mobile phone in the pocket of your client is very personal and attentive. This is a very simple weapon to apply, and the results are better long-term relationships with your prospects and customers.

23. Website content management

This weapon has one goal, and one goal only: to attract visitors back to your website time and time again. Soft steps are the way to Guerrilla profits. Gain consent to continue marketing, then proceed with regular soft steps to build rapport and maintain the Guerrilla attack.

There are literally millions of websites out there, and designers are getting more creative by the day. The problem is that designers very often know little about marketing. Creativity does not always equal profits.

One of the most profitable online weapons that I have tested is website content management. This is simply where you automatically vary the content of website pages. It's not rocket science, as there is plenty of software out there that can do this for you. All you have to do is supply the content, and the software manages the placement of copy and images.

So why would you want to vary the content so often? In short, to maintain interest. Regardless of what you have been told by others, when people visit your website they seek information. Furthermore, if the information has value, visitors will stay at your site longer, and the longer they stay, the longer they are exposed to your marketing messages.

This weapon does require some investment and some technical expertise, but nothing that cannot be mastered in a very short time. Consider the investment, because as we continue through this millennium your online business strategies will become more important than ever before.

24. Ego-free website

This may seem to contradict long-established Guerrilla Marketing teaching, as I have always said that Guerrillas need to have ego strength. This is still true today. A strong ego is very much a Guerrilla trait – however, your website is not the place to display your ego.

If you review your own website now, I'm willing to bet that your 'about us' page is one of the most copy-laden pages on your website. I'm also willing to wager that you refer to yourself more than to your prospects and customers. It's a very common story: more 'we', 'us' and 'our', than 'you' and 'yours'.

When a visitor lands on your website, they are seeking information with a mantra going through their mind, namely 'What's in it for me?' I accept that your organisation's history is important for some visitors, and your existing clients will be relevant for some visitors, too. However, to use your website to blow your own trumpet is not good use of an excellent resource. Once you have a visitor's attention, it should be your goal to show that visitor what you can do for their organisation – because believe me, that is the visitor's only interest.

All information should be presented as benefits for visitors. Give every single visitor a reason to choose to do business with you. Leave your ego at home and build your site for the convenience and gratification of the visitors that you so definitely seek.

25. 100 per cent opt-in list

Email is becoming a pain for everyone because there are so many organisations and individuals that abuse the system. I'm sure your inbox is packed full of spam. I know mine is.

Guerrillas do not spam anyone. Never, and not for any reason. I don't care how cheap the rented list is – it will not be profitable for you. There are a small number of reputable list rental companies who do operate strict 100 per cent opt-in policies, but these organisations are few and far between. The majority of list rental organisations (or more usually individuals) use a piece of software called a 'harvester'. This software searches through websites, forums, groups and domain registration sites capturing email addresses without the permission of the owners.

Using these email addresses can get you into large amounts of trouble. If your Internet service provider doesn't shut you down straightaway, then it will when it receives the thousands of spam complaints.

Guerrillas always use email in a professional manner. The best way to collect email addresses is not the quickest way, but it is one of the most responsible. When visitors land at your site, offer them some free information or a free product. In return, ask them for their name and email address. If your offering is high value you will be amazed at how many visitors will freely give their names and addresses. Now this is the important bit – don't abuse the trust that the visitor has shown you. In each and every future email communication you have with that visitor, offer them the opportunity to opt out and receive no further emails from you. If the visitor chooses to opt out they were not that committed to your message, and the chances are that a sale was unlikely anyway.

In modern Guerrilla Marketing we have a simple rule regarding contacting prospects and customers. Only contact prospects and customers when you have something *new* to say. Bring value to *every* communication.

'Touching base', 'calling to see what's happening' and 'making a quick call to catch up' does not offer any value to the prospect or customer. However, if you email with press releases or call with news of a new case study similar to that prospect or customer, then suddenly you are bringing value to the contact.

So once you have set up your website to give free articles, ebooks or whatever you have chosen, you will begin to collect freely offered email addresses. What do you do with this list of email addresses? You guard it with your life. It is the most valuable asset your company has. Email marketing is free, and the larger your list of 100 per cent opt-in email addresses, the more people you can market to – for free. You'll be surprised how quickly your list grows. In just six months the Guerrilla Marketing UK website collected 27,600 freely given names and email addresses, and based on the results of my clients, that is not exceptional.

Forget buying or renting email lists from third parties. Even if the vendor claims that the list is full of people who have agreed to accept email, those people have *not* agreed to receive emails from you.

Your 100 per cent opt-in email list will become the backbone of your online marketing, so make sure you do it right from day one. Build the list yourself using responsible Guerrilla Marketing methods and the power of this weapon will grow as the length of the list does.

You now have 25 new Guerrilla Marketing weapons to add to the existing list of 100 weapons. Better still, of the 25 new weapons, 18 are free to use. Let me clarify: you now have 18 new methods of creating profit and to apply them costs nothing.

Guerrilla Marketing weapons, or more specifically combinations of these weapons, are the reason why Guerrilla Marketing has been at the forefront of modern marketing for so many years. Most organisations that use traditional marketing only use a very small number of marketing weapons, often choosing to focus on advertising – which incidentally is the most expensive of all marketing weapons.

Guerrillas know that only combinations of weapons truly deliver consistency and predictability, plus sustainable, profitable growth. You now have the widest choice of weapons available to marketers today. Take them and choose which weapons you will use in your own marketing attack.

Be bold. Be aggressive. Be relentless. Launch your attack with your carefully selected weapons and commit to the attack.

The Future of Guerrilla Marketing

GUERRILLA MARKETING HAS LED the marketing industry for decades. This is because it is so unlike traditional marketing. If you come to one of my training courses I will show you 20 ways in which Guerrilla Marketing differs from traditional marketing – and I'm finding more differences all the time. The biggest difference, and I'm sure you've noticed it in this book, is that the goal of Guerrilla Marketing is profit. The only benchmark for your marketing should be profit. Traditional marketing places as much value on awards, brand awareness and peer recognition as it does on profit. Let me be very clear: a marketing campaign is only successful if it creates profit.

If your marketing agency tells you that although you didn't create any profit you did 'raise brand awareness', change your agency. If they tell you that the awards won by your campaign show that 'the market really related to the brand', ask them why the market didn't buy. If your campaign is not profitable, it is not successful. End of story.

Previous Guerrilla Marketing books have likened a Guerrilla Marketer to a stonecutter. The stonecutter knows that his first blow is unlikely to break the stone open, but he also knows that every single blow plays its part in the breaking process. Sometimes it may only take five or six well-placed strikes, while at other times it may take 200 or 300, yet the stonecutter never stops the assault on the stone. This is the way a Guerrilla should think and operate. No single weapon is likely to break open the market. Instead, Guerrillas use multiple weapons and multiple attacks, knowing that each attack is helping to open the market.

Occasionally Guerrilla Marketers are tempted to fiddle with a profitable campaign, often due to peer pressure from non-Guerrillas, and very often to 'keep the marketing fresh'. Before you submit to peer pressure, consider this story about a stonecutter.

There was once a stonecutter who was dissatisfied with his job and position in life. One morning on the way to work he passed by a rich businessman's house. He saw the businessman's cars, large garden and beautiful house and said to himself, 'He must be so happy with all that power. I wish I was in his shoes.' Suddenly, as if by magic, and without explanation, he became the rich businessman! He enjoyed wealth and luxuries that he had never experienced before, and was indeed happy.

One afternoon a man from the Inland Revenue visited, and suddenly his wealth was hugely reduced. He said to himself, 'He is so powerful. I wish I was the man from the Inland Revenue.' Once again, as if by magic, he became the man he so envied.

The man went to work every day, visiting rich businessmen and using his powers where he needed to do so. One afternoon he was uncomfortably hot and looked up at the sun. He thought to himself, 'The sun is so powerful. I wish I was the sun.' Again, without delay he became the sun.

He used his powers to heat the whole world, until one day a cloud blocked his rays from the Earth's surface. He looked down and thought, 'That cloud is more powerful than me. I wish I was that cloud.' Magically, he became the cloud.

Straightaway he realised that he had no control over his own movement, that he was completely reliant on the wind. 'How powerful the wind must be,' he thought. 'I wish I was the wind.' Suddenly, he became the wind.

He used his newfound powers to blow tiles off roofs, uproot trees and control clouds, until he noticed something that would not move, no matter how forcefully he blew against it. That thing was a huge stone.

He thought to himself, 'That stone is more powerful than me. I wish I was that stone.' He felt complete, safe in the knowledge that he was now more powerful than anything else on Earth. Soon, he heard the sound of a hammer and chisel, and felt himself being changed.

He thought, 'What could be more powerful than I, the stone?' And then he saw . . . a stonecutter.

Your marketing plan, with the commitment of you and your colleagues, will succeed, providing you have applied the time-proven Guerrilla Marketing principles and have patience.

The people surrounding you may tell you that you need to change your marketing campaign, to 'keep it fresh' or to 'try something new'. Both of these reasons are fine for changing a campaign, but you should not change it if it is working profitably. There is no problem with testing small adjustments to see if they improve profitability, but remember that the market is very sensitive to change, and many people feel that a change in your marketing will add to the perceived risk. After all, they're comfortable with your present identity and message. It has taken time, but they are now comfortable. If you make changes now, will they still remain comfortable with your message and identity? You need to test your changes to find out.

The evolution of Guerrilla Marketing

Guerrilla Marketing has always championed change. Recently, I've looked hard at Guerrilla Marketing itself. I researched our strategies and weapons, and I contacted many of my clients to ask for their feedback. What I found was that to continue leading the marketing industry, Guerrilla Marketing needs to evolve more quickly than traditional marketing. The industry is changing rapidly, and traditional marketing is failing to keep up. That must not happen to Guerrilla Marketing.

This book is the first step in the evolution of Guerrilla Marketing. Although Guerrilla Marketing has naturally evolved over the past few decades, the natural evolution is simply not quick enough to maintain position at the forefront of modern marketing methods and strategies. Therefore, I've decided to speed the evolution of Guerrilla Marketing by personally injecting new methods, strategies, weapons and sciences into our already bulging arsenal. The good news for Guerrillas everywhere is that it does not stop there. I have committed, and now wish to document, my intention to allocate sufficient resources to ensure the ongoing accelerated evolution of Guerrilla Marketing.

It is my goal to maintain our market leading position, as I believe it is important for Guerrilla Marketing to do this. To ensure our dominant market position, and to drive the evolution of Guerrilla Marketing, I have identified seven action items:

1. Continuing to provide the most advanced and consistently profitable marketing expertise to our clients.

2. Identifying and developing new weapons.

3. Improving the performance of existing weapons.

4. Working with partners to identify and detail new strategies.

5. Using the feedback of Guerrilla Marketing Association members to further develop new and existing Guerrilla Marketing strategies.

6. Using the feedback of our clients to develop marketing weapons and strategies that are needed in the modern marketing industry.

7. Continue to write Guerrilla Marketing books, providing anyone and everyone with profit-based Guerrilla Marketing strategies.

Preserving the core beliefs of Guerrilla Marketing

Throughout the evolution the key beliefs of Guerrilla Marketing must be preserved. Although I accept that Guerrilla Marketing must change to maintain its market-leading status, I absolutely will not compromise on certain values and beliefs:

- Marketing is only successful if it is profitable. Profit is the *only* benchmark for marketing.

- Marketing should be driven by psychology, neurology and physiology. Opinions and experience are aids, but not the basis for profitable marketing strategies.

- Marketing should be directed at the unconscious mind of your prospects and customers.

- Creativity is not a replacement for a marketing message, and creativity is a result of hard work – not genetics.

- Motivating prospects and customers with pain is not responsible marketing. Guerrillas want customers to experience 'purchase bliss' not 'buyer's remorse'.

- A 100 per cent opt-in list is the *only* email list you should ever use.

- Single marketing weapons do not work well. Guerrillas create campaigns that utilise combinations of weapons.

- Marketing should be an interactive dialogue, not a monologue.

- Marketing does not need to be expensive.

These core beliefs, which have been explored in this book, form the foundation of modern Guerrilla Marketing, and will continue to do so far into the future. Guerrilla Marketing will always focus on your application of time, effort and imagination, and not on the need for a large marketing budget.

The function of creativity

Sometimes my clients tell me, 'I'm just not creative,' or 'I'm more logical than I am creative.' Creativity is very often misunderstood. Albert Einstein was a genius, perhaps the greatest genius ever, and yet he is not usually considered creative.

Einstein was a clerk in the patent office. Unfortunately, he found the job to be boring and repetitive. As a result, he had plenty of time to think and daydream. One evening on the way home, as he sat on the slow-moving tram, he looked out and saw a clock tower. As the tram slowly pulled away from the clock tower he wondered what would happen if the tram moved away from the clock tower at the speed of light. He determined that for him, the time on the clock face would appear to have stopped. However, he also concluded that the time on his own watch would appear to continue correctly, as it would be travelling with him at the speed of light – and so the theory of relativity was established (or at least the foundations of the theory.)

Creativity and imagination are naturally found in all humans. It is why birds build cold, draughty nests each year, while I live in a house with central heating, a broadband Internet connection and satellite TV. Guerrillas know that utilising creativity and imagination can save hundreds, thousands or even millions of pounds in marketing budgets. When I work with my clients, it is always my goal to help them find more profitable ways to do what they want or need to do. That often requires creative thinking.

Let me be clear: I don't consider myself to be particularly creative. However, what creativity I do have comes from experience, knowledge and my ability to think original thoughts – without limitation. That is my strength. I approach/problems with a simple mantra, 'I'm not quitting until I get the answer.' I've modelled Einstein in that approach. He would often lock himself in a room with a problem. He would refuse any interruption, including food and drink, and was occasionally known to work for 24 hours or more without a break. His only goal was the answer.

I don't go to quite those extremes, but I do concentrate entirely on a problem and refuse to accept any answer that my mind might offer, until I'm positive it is the best possible solution. Try it – it may work for you, too.

The simplicity of marketing

Marketing is very simple. You should aim to use communications expertise to clearly present your benefit, or benefits, in a positive manner to a focused audience. Take care when you read that last sentence, as it has a number of key points therein.

'communications expertise'

The methods and strategies presented to you in this book are not intended to trick clients. This is not stealth marketing. All the material in this book is designed to make your marketing message (the thrust) better understood. Guerrilla Marketing does not lend itself to misleading prospects or customers, as Guerrillas view each contact as a possible partner. In earlier chapters I described Guerrilla Marketing as similar to trying to woo a desired partner of the opposite sex. If you trick someone into a relationship, does that relationship have solid enough foundations to stand the test of time? I doubt it.

'clearly present'

When I first review my clients' marketing materials, more often than not I find that the marketing message and the benefits are not clear. Typically this is because the marketing department that wrote the copy has a full and thorough understanding of the product or services and related benefits, and simply takes it for granted that all readers do, too.

Never assume that the reader of your marketing collateral has the same level of expertise as yourself. Present benefits in their most basic form. It could be that the purchasing decision will be made by the finance department, in which case pure profitability may be the motivating factor. On the flipside of that argument, the purchasing decision may be made by the sales director, in which case their motivating driver may be improving the time-management performance of the department. You simply can't be sure, and you can't be the man for all seasons, so the only way to present your message is as clearly and simply as possible.

'in a positive manner'

I believe I have made my position clear about the fact that marketing should not focus on creating negative states in prospects and customers. Creating and then developing negative states, as in the traditional 'pain' method (see page 53), does not leave the prospect or customer in a resourceful state. When I'm with someone who is about to make a purchasing decision, I want that person to be in the most resourceful state that I can possibly arouse. Then, after the purchasing decision is made, the purchaser remains content and excited about the purchase. That, in turn, is likely to bring repeat business and referrals. I'll leave this topic there – but watch this space, as this is a subject that will be expanded upon in future Guerrilla Marketing books.

'focused audience'

Guerrillas know that the most profits come from marketing to people who have consented to receive your marketing materials. Blanket marketing to people who have no desire or motivation to receive your materials is a much more expensive marketing campaign, as the audience typically requires more presentations of your message, to move them from apathy to the purchasing decision. Identifying a focused audience, and then marketing to that audience with laser precision and ruthless consistency, is the way of the Guerrilla.

The future role of NLP in Guerrilla Marketing

As you have now seen in this book, Guerrilla Marketing is gaining pace in developing advanced, profitable marketing strategies and weapons. One of the differences between Guerrilla Marketing and traditional marketing has always been that traditional marketing focuses on subjective opinions and experience, whereas Guerrilla Marketing prefers to utilise psychology and other sciences surrounding human nature. I now want to add Neurolinguistic Programming (NLP) to that selection of sciences.

NLP is now time-proven. Dr Bandler and Dr Grinder first introduced NLP in the early 1970s, and over the past 30 years the results that they, and thousands of other practitioners, have achieved are astounding. As is the case with Guerrilla Marketing, NLP is evolving and the creators are driving the evolution. NLP offers a huge selection of tools that we can apply in Guerrilla Marketing, and I intend to do so.

The future

So where does Guerrilla Marketing go from here? As stated, my intention is that we create better weapons, develop even more profitable strategies and continue to lead the marketing world. I'm a pragmatist. My interest is in methods and strategies that create and sustain profit. The offerings in this book are not just theories. They are the cream of present-day Guerrilla Marketing – and remember this is only the beginning of the evolution. I've presented you with 25 new weapons, and I've barely scratched the surface. There are even more weapons coming your way in the very near future, and in true Guerrilla fashion many of them will be weapons that are free to deploy.

Some of the methods described in this book are very advanced in their nature, and yet simple to use. That is a trend that will continue throughout the evolution. I like advanced weapons if they bring profit, but I have no interest in confusing anybody. Guerrilla Marketing has always sought to demystify marketing, not make it even more of a labyrinth. There are too many marketing books on the shelves already that promise to present 'secrets' that 'guarantee' your success. There are even more emails bouncing around that make the same promises. I've said it before, and I'll say it one more time: there are no secrets.

Guerrilla Marketing was originally developed to enable small businesses to directly compete with large multinational organisations. That is the root of Guerrilla Marketing, and that will never be forgotten. The strategies, techniques and weapons that are created over the next few years will always be made available to small businesses, not just for the sake of Guerrilla Marketing roots, but also because there are now more small businesses than ever before. There has never been a better time for Guerrilla Marketing to flourish. The ugliness of today's world economy is exactly the reason why Guerrilla Marketing is more popular than ever. I have clients across the globe, from the UK across the whole of Europe to Russia, as far south as Cape Town and many organisations in the US. Guerrilla Marketing is multicultural because it focuses on people and profit. The information in this book can be applied in almost any country – even the language patterns are designed to work across many cultures.

This book is packed full of profit creating strategies, methods and weapons. Some of the material is more complex than anything I've presented before, and I've increased its pace compared to my previous books and given you more new weapons and strategies than ever before. Do not be afraid to experiment and test – I do it all the time.

My next book will be even harder hitting, packed full of even more weapons, more effective language patterns, and will bring you to the edge of the envelope. I'm pushing Guerrilla Marketing harder than ever before. I'm squeezing every molecule of profit that I can find from every single weapon I can devise. I'm increasing the precision persuasion in the language that we use and working on perfecting the strategies that have always performed well. Remember, this is not just about new material. Guerrilla Marketing has a pedigree that is envied the world over.

Guerrilla Marketing is moving faster than ever before, and it's still gaining pace. I have no intention of stopping the acceleration. I will make existing material better and more profitable, and I'll work with partners to create new and exciting strategies that create profits at levels previously considered fantasy. This is the future of Guerrilla Marketing.

Traditional marketing no longer produces consistency or predictability. Commerce needs something new, as organisations thirst for profit. Guerrilla Marketing brings what is needed most: profits through sound marketing strategies and the determination to act upon proven methods and weapons.

I've raised the stakes.

I'm increasing the pace.

I have the weapons I need.

I refuse to turn back.

Welcome to the Guerrilla Marketing Revolution.

Resources

- *Guerrilla Marketing* – Jay Conrad Levinson; Houghton Mifflin, 1985

- *Guerrilla Marketing Attack* – Jay Conrad Levinson; Houghton Mifflin, 1990

- *Encyclopaedia of Systemic NLP and NLP New Coding* – Robert Dilts & Judith DeLozier; NLP University Press, 2000

- *Persuasion Engineering* – Dr Richard Bandler & John LaValle; Meta Publications, 1995

- *Usability News* – Software Usability Research Laboratory (SURL) Wichita State University; http://www.usabilitynews.com

- *Fibonacci Numbers and The Golden Section* – Dr Ron Knott; http://www.mcs.surrey.ac.uk/Personal/R.Knott/Fibonacci /fib.html

- *Time for a Change* – Dr Richard Bandler; Meta Publications, 1993

- *The Cynics Guide* to NLP – Irish Institute of NLP; http://www.nlp.ie/cynics.htm

- *Educating is a verb not a noun* – Anton Raps;
  http://www.nlp.ie/educ.htm

For more information on Guerrilla Marketing visit:
www.guerrillamarketinginternational.co.uk

Index